SOMETHING BEAUTIFUL
OUT *of* ME

MARQUETA PLUM JENKINS

ACKNOWLEDGEMENTS

Who would've ever thought I would be here and now, still in the land of the living? Between the attempts made on my life from the enemy of my soul to my thoughts of wanting to take my own life from time to time, I'm so glad I made it, and I can't do anything but give God all of the glory, the honor, the praise and certainly every ounce of credit. I am NOTHING without Him!

To the God of ALL creation, where would I be without you? Where would I be without your grace and mercy? Your unfailing love for me? Your unconditional forgiveness towards me hourly … daily … weekly … yearly? If I had a thousand, no, a million tongues, it still wouldn't be enough to thank you for all that you have done for me, in me, through me. I am so grateful for you being a way-maker, miracle-worker, promise-keeper and a light in the darkness. Thank you for being true to your word and never leaving me, nor forsaking me. Thank you for your patience with me when I mess up big time, when I'm disobedient, stubborn or just being a plain ol' ratchet, hot mess. Thank you for instilling purpose inside of me and not letting me die before my time. Thank you for the level of greatness you have planted in me; then you have the audacity to believe in me? Wow. I am in complete and utter awe. I could go on and on simply because you have been just … that … good. Lastly, thank you for being the ONE who never leaves the one behind.

To my mom, Jacquelyn Renee Hewitt, you are every Marvel comic hero in my book. Your strength, resilience, fortitude and desire to keep going even when you had nothing left to fight with… I could never come close in comparison. If people really knew how the Lord truly kept you, they would know where I get just a small percentage of these character traits from. Thank you for every prayer even when my outcome looked bleak. I only hope that you see a glimmer of you in me.

To my six heartbeats… Dachon Negron, A'Chanti Negron, Stefon Negron, Marreon Negron, Yoshua Harris and Israel Harris. You are the very reason why I live and the strength I need to keep striving. I go hard in the paint because I look forward to the day I have made each of you proud of me.

To my sibs (maternal) Danny Negron, Sommer Graves (Peter), Timothy Negron (Shani) and Anthony Negron… Thank you for your endurance, patience and love during the most difficult years of my life. I pray that God blesses you a thousandfold for everything you have done and for just being there. (Paternal) Deneen Majors, Jason Hardy (d) 1974–2001, Joe Plum Jr, and Antonio Plum. I love you deeply. To the Jenkins, Futrell and Plum families, I am honored to come from such great stock.

To Tiffany "Tip" Ravanell… I did it, sis. Apostle Torian A. Patterson, I kept my promise to you, and I pray that you both continue to Rest in Perfection until we meet again. Special shoutout to my godmother Francine Locker, and to my entire Berkley family and crew from the Boondocks to the Berkley Rec Center, to Sumler Terrace and Bell Diamond… There are too many of y'all to name, but y'all already know the count with me! We lead the way, we're the first to do the most, and we produce nothing but the best. I love y'all for real and forever. It's only up from here!!

CONTENTS

INTRODUCTION

I know without a shadow of a doubt that I should not be alive today. What makes this statement so bold is that currently the entire world is dealing with a pandemic. It's October 2020 and COVID-19 cases are STILL popping up all over; people are continuously passing away, yet my God obviously still has a need for me because I'm here, writing this testimony to those who have an ear to hear. If Abba, the Great I am that I Am, can use me (flaws and all) then surely He can use anyone willing to surrender their will in order for His to be fulfilled.

Have you ever wondered why people go through so much in life? You start asking yourself questions like, *What in the world did he or she do to suffer like that? Who in the world did they piss off because they really got it out for them?* Well, that would be me. I asked those same questions because I was going through what seemed like hell every day. I mean I couldn't catch a break if someone threw it at me! Things were so bad at one time, I really thought I was sent to Earth just to have "bad luck" find me. I even began speaking this out loud, but I didn't know the power my words had because what I spoke literally started to happen—more so than what was already occurring—and it drove me to the point of wanting to end my life several times. The suffering was just that bad!

I started questioning my purpose for even living: Did I have a purpose besides being a poster child for bad luck? What was my purpose? Anything had to be better than what life had portrayed itself to be, especially for the last 37 years. Yep, you read that right. Seems like a long time, huh? Three decades of dealing with loss, struggle, financial despair, a bad reputation, low self-esteem, and no self-worth or self-respect. But in the midst of it all, something deep down inside was anchored to hope. It was holding on for dear life just in case tomorrow was the day my life would change forever, only for tomorrow to come and go with little to no change.

Little did I know that God was creating, shaping and molding me into something so beautiful that the eyes of the beholder wouldn't be able to stand the brilliance of the beauty resonating from within me, and it would eventually showcase exactly what He created, shaped and formed me to be.

How could anything good come from the broken, fragmented pieces that consisted of me? I was spiritually, emotionally and mentally shattered into a million pieces, yet God took His ever-loving time to put me back together, omitting the pieces that were never supposed to be part of who I am. This masterpiece in the making will prove that His love conquers and covers all and in spite of the decisions we make, for it's all a part of our journey. If you really know our Heavenly Father, the God of all creation, then you are aware that nothing catches Him by surprise. He already knows our thoughts before we think them; surely, He knows what we're going to do before we do it and He STILL forgives us and loves us right in the middle of our mess. Wow! What kind of God do we serve who loves us past our faults and flaws? In order for "Something Beautiful" to be made out of me, I have to bare my soul and share my story of the good, the bad, the ugly and the indifferent. Despite everything I hated and despised about myself, God loved me through it all. He always knew what I would become and now you will as well.

Chapter 1

I KNEW I WAS DIFFERENT

Ever since I was seven years old, I knew that I was different. I didn't know it at the time, but when I look back over my life, I can pinpoint that that was the very age when I stood out. I was never meant to fit in because I was set apart from others. I remember being asked what I wanted to be when I grew up. I had so much personality; everyone just knew I would be some type of entertainer. I simply said I wanted to be a stockbroker, which was strange because I had no point of reference to even know what a stockbroker was, what they did or what this career looked like. My parents did not have a television during the majority of my younger years so where did this idea originate?

All I did was read. I had an insatiable appetite for knowledge and feeding my brain, so I read everything I could get my hands on, hence the reason why my imagination was so vivid. There was nothing else to do since my siblings were too young to play with at that time, so reading became my favorite pastime and the characters in the books were my friends. I had playmates that lived close by, but my mother had very strict rules: I had to be in the house by a certain time, I couldn't go around the corner of my block and I definitely couldn't go into anyone's house without permission. My friends' parents weren't as strict and this led to me being left out of a lot of activities.

I didn't understand at the time why there was such strict protection over me, but I found myself instilling the same rules in my household when I started having children. My overprotection came from being molested when I was around 10 years old and also after being sexually assaulted while serving on active duty. It was not until I was older that I discovered something similar happened to my mother, allowing the onset of "generational cycles" to continue. "What is this?" I'm glad you asked. Allow me to segue for a moment in order to bring clarity and understanding to some areas that need light shed upon them.

People must understand there is an unseen realm operating in real time, often appearing in the natural. Many phenomena occur without explanation, unless you are familiar with what has taken place and where it comes from. I am referring to angels, spirits and invisible activity. Whether you agree or not, it is very real and if you haven't experienced it yet, don't worry … you will.

"Generational curses or cycles" are part of the unseen activity that appears in the natural. What do I mean by this? Examples are sicknesses that run rampant in women and men, like various types of cancer can be a cursed cycle. Women who marry and divorce several times are in a cursed cycle. Or what happened to me and my mother (rape and molestation) when it happens to kids and adults on a regular basis. Absent parents, abusive mothers and fathers, alcoholics and addicts, physical, sexual, mental and emotional abusers … the list goes on and on, but they all stem from cursed cycles. A cycle is something that is repeated: someone started it and others continued it.

You can't visibly see that it's been passed down, but eventually it will manifest itself in the actions portrayed by those closest to us. Maybe it started with your great-grandparents; then their children dealt with it, and their grandchildren, etc. The behavior continues to pass down generationally until someone recognizes it and counteracts to break the curse and cycle.

This is done by (1) recognizing the issue or problem, (2) verbally affirming into the atmosphere that the curse or cycle stops with you, and (3) physically taking action to do whatever is necessary to completely bring these things to a screeching halt. If it's sickness then you can prevent it by getting checkups, changing your eating habits, exercising and practicing a healthy lifestyle. Or if you witnessed abuse and find yourself displaying abusive tendencies towards your loved ones, seek counseling. Never be ashamed to ask for help, and don't beat yourself when you make mistakes. We're not perfect, nor will we ever be, but it doesn't give us an excuse for doing what we want whenever we want to for everything has cause and effect, it has repercussions, or it comes full circle.

Life doesn't come with a manual; nor are we forewarned about anything that previously took place in our family tree. It takes someone like me to go through years of searching and questioning the whys of life so that I can share it with those who are destined to read this book and provide the answers they have been desperately seeking. Now that you know the why, you will no longer be ignorant to what's going on in your life, and you can start making a change today. You have way more power than you know, and this is how you find out just how much lies in you!

Whew... I know that was a lot to say, and a bit heavy, but it was necessary. It might have even blown over someone's head, but I felt the need to say it then explain. I chose this chapter to put this revelation in because it will help you to understand why my life went the route that it did and eventually understand folks like me more. It is also my belief that the right reader will not only see that they're not alone in this thing called life, and that someone else has been or is going through the same things they're going through even now, but most importantly they will know that there is yet hope and they will get through these tough and difficult times.

All you need is one lightbulb moment, and your life can change forever. Well, here it is! God is so loving, thoughtful and caring that He chooses one or more persons in families to "anoint" with the power to break cycles and curses. They're often the weird, quirky ones who don't quite fit the family status quo, or the most popular term is "black sheep" of the family. It is typical of them to be rejected, picked on, treated differently, and often left out because they're bothersome. Sounds familiar? Yeah, we all have one or more of them in our family, and more than likely, that's your family's curse/cycle breaker.

Let's go deeper: they have been equipped with "spiritual gifts" used as "weapons" in order to carry out the assignment of shifting and changing the trajectory of a family's lineage and direction in life journey. But these gifts don't come cheaply, nor are they free. Think of who I just described in your family. It could be you, a cousin, aunt, or uncle ... anybody. Can you imagine the ridicule, the shaming, name-calling and bullying they deal or dealt with yet had no earthly clue as to why? We are considered "gifts with giftings." The price we pay in order to operate in these giftings is so crucial that the thought of being dead brings more comfort than living in what feels like daily torture; however, the reward for enduring far outweighs what the Bible calls "temporary suffering".

All of what I described is who I am and it has shaped my life overall. It took many years to understand why I went through hell and back several times because this is not a "one and done" deal. Oh no! There is a price to pay for the life we are called to live. But it is a beautiful exchange for the joy that comes with knowing we have fulfilled our purpose in life. Yes, it seems counterproductive because who really asks to be born? We don't get to choose our birth parents and families, and we don't get to choose the hand that life deals us. However, we do get to choose the path life or death sets before us in lieu of the life we are given. It's all about how you react to situations and circumstances that are bound to happen and how you respond based on these actions will determine what's next.

Chapter 2

WHAT WAS NEXT FOR ME

What was next for me was the actual training and preparation for how God intended to use my life. As I stated earlier, I was raised in a Christian home. All I knew was God, church and school. We stayed in church so much throughout the week I felt like it was my second home. Then both my parents were leaders in the church, so the schedule went like this:

- Sunday School
- Sunday Morning Service
- Parents lingered around for an hour talking
- Went home for dinner then back to church
- Sunday Evening Service
- Monday evening – prayer room duty
- Tuesday evening – leadership meeting
- Wednesday evening – Bible study
- Thursday – whatever ministry needed assistance
- Friday – special guest service, concert, play, etc.

- Saturday – volunteer to clean up the sanctuary
- Back to church early that following Sunday (Good grief, Charlie Brown!)

This continued for years unless extenuating circumstances like the weather or some other emergency kept us from making an appearance. It was fun when I was a kid because I loved being in the presence of God, but as I got older it started interfering with me being a moody teen, who wanted to be alone in a room unbothered. It became a bit too much! I remember sitting on the side of my bed just over it and thinking to myself, *You know, maybe going to hell ain't such a bad idea after all!* LOL, it's funny now, but it wasn't funny back then. Oh yeah, did I also mention that I attended school at this same church? I told my mom maybe I should just get a sleeping bag and stay at the church since I was always there. Yeah, that didn't go over too well. I can still feel the sting of the slap on my lips. My mom was generally soft-spoken and gentle with her words, but she was something else behind closed doors with the whippin's!

I remember her telling me that I asked to give my life to Christ at the tender age of six and was filled with the Holy Spirit that same night. I believe an impartation and activation took place as well, in which I was given the gifts in which I'm operating in today. Back then, I didn't know what anything was, what I possessed, and actually didn't learn of them until years later. I then had to be taught how to use them. The gifts that I speak of are the fivefold ministry: Apostle, Prophet, Evangelist, Pastor or Teacher. These gifts and callings are given "without repentance"—meaning whether or not you choose to do what you are gifted and/or called to do, God doesn't take the gift or calling back.

My gift in this case is prophetic, which is the ability to receive a divinely inspired message and deliver it to others in the church or whoever God allows me to meet outside of church. According to the Bible, these messages can take the form of exhortation, correction, disclosure of secret sins, prediction of future events, comfort, inspiration or other revelations given to equip and edify the body of Christ. (*1 Cor 14:3–4, 24–25*)

When I reflect over my life now, I understand why I was always very compassionate and caring towards other people. Why I always wanted to comfort those who were sad or down and would find the words flowing out of my mouth to give them life and put a smile on their face. Why I loved so deep and hard, because I could feel the hurt and pain being dealt with; sometimes I would have visions of what they were secretly going through and all I could do was cry because I felt like there was nothing I could do to stop it. I didn't really know how to pray with power as I only knew the surface prayers which covered me when I went to bed. You know the one I'm talking about:

Now I lay me down to sleep.

I pray the Lord my soul to keep.

If I should die before I wake,

I pray the Lord my soul to take.

I didn't discover the intercessory prayer warrior I am now until the surface prayers weren't cutting it anymore. I had to start digging deep because the situations I was in required a level of crying out that only erupts from anguish.

I also saw or knew things before they happened and sometimes I spoke what I knew or saw with confidence; then, when it happened, people looked at me wondering how I knew it would occur. I would always say I didn't know because, honestly, I didn't. Again, it wasn't until later on that I was mature enough to understand that which came easily to me—but by that time I had already been through so much; I would have preferred to return the gift or have it taken had I known all the hardship it included.

Chapter 3

TRAPS SET BY THE ENEMY

When it comes to the enemy of our soul, he is shrewd and very cunning. Not giving him any type of credit, but I recall the Holy Spirit told me years ago that I needed to "study my enemy(s)." That meant identify traps set by the enemy; how he operated, what tools and tactics he used to accomplish his evil deeds. He loves no one but himself. He's a liar and the truth is nowhere in him. He makes these traps glitter like gold so when you touch them, you get gold dust on your fingers and on different parts of your body.

When you touch your head, he plants seeds of fear, doubt, worry and frustration in your mind.

When you touch your eyes, things appear to be attractive and look so good you will go to great lengths to own them, possess them and make them yours no matter what.

When you touch your private areas, the gold dust awakens the lustful desires of wanting love however you can get it; giving it away wantonly, sparing no cost—not even if it costs you your life.

Gold flecks fall to our feet, urging, pulling and pushing us to run swiftly towards acts and deeds that are morally and ethically wrong—but we're drawn to do them anyway. This gold dust shimmers and shines brilliantly and brightly when the light reflects on it, so you can't help but desire it more than air, more than life itself. But it's merely a distraction, a ruse to get you to open the door to the Pandora's Box of ill-fated consequences lying in wait to devour unsuspecting victims—me and you, our family members, friends and loved ones.

The traps designed for me were indeed meant to annihilate me, destroy me and completely obliterate me from the face of the earth because of my pure desire to love and live for God. I had an experience at the altar of Rock Church in Virginia Beach, VA around the year 1980, at an age when most only know about dolls, toys, candy and food. I had an encounter with God in which an exchange occurred. See, my mother was the one who God placed His thumbprint on; the one who would evangelize the gospel to our family of non-believers and because she surrendered her life to Christ, her seeds (children) were blessed with spiritual and natural gifts in exchange for her "yes" to salvation.

While at the altar, I can only imagine that a war was waged against me, for I know the enemy had a glimpse of my future. He was privy to information I had yet to discover. He had the drop on me and started fighting me before I could even learn how to fight. He set traps designed to take down giants in the faith because that's how BIG and BRIGHT this future of mine was, and yet at one point in my life, I couldn't tell you if I was going to continue living to remotely see the light of day.

By the age of 10 I was touched, fondled and partially penetrated by a cousin, yet I didn't know that what had happened was wrong on so many levels, and, quite honestly, I don't think they did either. I didn't know my body was a temple and that it was to stay in virgin mode until I was married. I didn't have a clue as to what "inappropriate touching" was because I wasn't around people like that, so it wasn't deemed necessary until I was of age to have "the talk". My mother did an excellent job of protecting me from predators in the neighborhood—but what do you do when you're innocently playing house with older cousins who don't know how to handle frequent erections? Obviously, they saw some type of an example of what do with their manhood and where to put it, but maybe no one explained that you don't practice with a female, blood-related cousin. See how the enemy innocently introduces incest through these types of games? I also never said anything about it until I was older, but I carried a cloak of shame that didn't appear until later.

This was trap root #1 – *shame, guilt, condemnation*
and feeling dirty.

By the age of 12, I noticed how physically different I looked compared to my siblings and started to question why. I'm sure my mom was hoping I would never notice, but there wasn't much that got past me. I was gifted with a high level of intelligence; I had more book smarts than common sense but was far from a dummy. I began a barrage of questions like, "Why am I darker than them? Why is their hair softer and curlier than mine? What do my cousins mean by, 'That's not your real dad'? What did the other kids mean when they asked me what my brothers and sister were 'mixed with'?" I was so green, so naïve you could've bought me for a penny with a lot of stuff—yet somehow, I still seemed to perceive a lot and didn't know how or why.

Long story short, the father I had growing up was not my biological father. He met my mother when I was five, married her when I was six—adopting me in the process—and gave me his last name. He was Puerto Rican, and my mother is Black, so you already know that mixture alone produced beautiful children with gorgeous hair and complexions.

However, my biological father is Native American and Black, and I was blessed with his prominent cheekbones, full lips and nice grade of hair that is just as beautiful when heat is applied. My exotic looks didn't start to appear until I was a teenager, but I felt ugly as a kid because I was noticeably different. I didn't meet him until I was in my early twenties, but the way God orchestrated that further let me know just how mindful He is of me. I will talk about meeting him, my other siblings and my paternal side of the family later on.

Don't get me wrong; my stepfather loved me and treated me like I was his own and never referred to me as his stepdaughter, but the thoughts and questions about who my real dad was went unanswered mostly because I asked questions at the wrong time and typically when I got into some sort of trouble. I did not know that I was allowing a trait of spitefulness to operate within me, causing hurt and pain to those who loved me—but things were being said by other kids and family members that I didn't know how to process, nor did I know how to answer them, so it made me feel like I didn't belong.

Trap root #2 was – *rejection, feeling like I wasn't good enough and that something was wrong with me.*

Chapter 4

SCHOOL OF HARD KNOCKS

The School of Hard Knocks; an idiomatic phrase meaning the sometimes painful education one gets from life's negative experiences. To learn something, usually a life lesson, the hard way often by way of mistakes and poor choices.

I was inducted into this school sooner than I thought, whether I wanted to attend or not. Voluntarily or involuntarily, I was made a student and forced to sit in the front row with perfect attendance. This is probably one of the few places where everyone is a straight A, honor roll student because, whether you like it or not, you will pass each and every test or retake it until you pass with flying colors. There's an indefinite unspoken rule and probably the only rule: Life is a series of tests; you will take each and every one or you will not pass GO until you do.

SOHK First lesson: *The Black culture is a movement.*
Get in where you fit in.

My hair was thick, untamed, and I was extremely tender-headed, so my mom dreaded doing my hair. Whatever she was able to do without me crying as if she was killing me was the style I wore for the day. It was okay when I was in elementary school because the private school I attended was predominantly white.

They didn't know about the black culture, about how our hair was our crowning glory and should always look as such. They didn't know that we have a swag out of this world that has often been imitated but never duplicated. We are in a class all by ourselves and it is a privilege and an honor to be of the Black race. However, at this particular time, I was oblivious to my heritage and so were my classmates. They didn't know any better (neither did I); therefore, I was none the wiser of what I didn't know, yet somehow life was still good. That was until my scholarship ran out, funds were no longer available to pay out of pocket and my parents had to make the painful decision to put me in a public school. A predominantly *black* public school I might add.

Around the same time, my parents bought a house big enough for a family of seven; five kids, two adults and off and on family members would stay in the side apartment connected to the house. That was great as we had more space to run and play, but the issue was that it was in a rough neighborhood. We moved from the quiet, whimsical Crown Point area in Norfolk, VA to a rough and tumble section of South Norfolk (Berkley to be exact) and that's when my life changed.

Talk about a culture shock. My clothes were nowhere near as nice as the other middle-schoolers, and I had no idea that other black kids wore such elaborate styles with their hair. There was a range of relaxers, mushroom styles, rat tails and shags. I saw an array of labels I had never heard of like GUESS, Nike, Adidas, Lacoste, Pepsi Cola shirts, Levi Jeans—you name it they wore it. I was used to wearing a uniform every day and when not in uniform I had my play clothes that I wore on the weekend.

Life was about to make its debut and if Kevin Hart was a comedian then, I would be saying in his voice, *"Nooo ... she wasn't ready! I'm not ready."* I was bound to get caught up, no matter how much my parents instilled boundaries and rules within me. Nine times out of ten the environment always wins, and such was the case with me.

I felt like Rainbow from the show *Black-ish*; as a matter of fact, that is EXACTLY who I was at that time! The example couldn't be more perfect; a naïve, sheltered pre-teen nerd with untamed hair and no sense of style who was the target for bullies and the butt of jokes every single day. It was non-stop and since I didn't know how to joke back, it took a minute until I caught on; then I joked my own self so I could beat them to it. I laughed with them to keep from crying in public, which was a complete no-no.

Remember the tests I described earlier? You know; the ones you had to retake if you failed until you passed? Yeah, this was one of them. I was super-sensitive spiritually and was emotional in the natural because I was experiencing puberty at the same time, so I was catching hell both ways. Crying was a sign of weakness and I had to learn early on to suck it up until I got home. The choice was yours, but you had to choose wisely, otherwise you ended up getting smacked upside the head or got a "frog" by getting punched in the arm to toughen you up.

I finally got the hang of this middle school thing and even made a couple friends. I started to obtain an identity and really got to know myself. I hadn't realized how much my head was in the clouds until I started learning stuff I had no business learning at the age I was. This was due to my innocence being so apparent, so something had to be done to taint it even more.

When I was inside the house, I devoured every book I could get my hands on since we didn't have a television. I was also a tomboy, so climbing trees and playing in the dirt was my favorite pastime. I would run and sweat so hard I would smell like a musty mountain lion by the time I had to come in the house. I didn't dress like a boy, but I sure as heck didn't act like a girl when I had dresses on either. My dress shoes stayed scuffed up from playing so hard, and my stockings kept runs and holes in them. I even managed to tear up tights that were made like stockings with the ribbed design in them and wore the knees out too!

I had a way to go and grow, but I found some other outcasts who were just like me. We didn't fit in; all we cared about was schoolwork and books and seeing who could read the thickest novels. At that time Stephen King was gaining notoriety in our group, along with V.C. Andrews, and I was finally gaining my footing. But as life would have it, it rudely inserted a monkey-wrench into my seemingly "beginning-to-become-perfect-again" life.

SOHK Second Lesson: *Roll with the brick hard punches or get rolled over...Periodt!*

First fight: I was in the 8th grade and prided myself on finally getting the hang of the do's and don'ts, but apparently a few were missed. I don't know whose job it was to provide me with the rules, but clearly they failed. I thought I was doing something by sitting in the back of the bus with the juniors, seniors and other popular kids. Man, you couldn't tell me I wasn't the cool kid on the block. In my effort to fit into my new environment, I joined in the friendly banter of jokes and whatever else met our folly.

Here's another rule: don't laugh too hard at the jokes, especially if there is something about you to be joked or you end up with the bull's-eye target on your back. Again, I didn't get the memo and apparently I laughed a little too hard like I was at a comedy show at the Funny Bone! Oh yeah, here's another rule that someone forgot to school me on *inserting an eye roll*—you never, EVER … ever, ever, ever, ever, ever … tell a "yo momma" joke if you have not earned your spot to do so. EVER! I mean your comeback jokes gotta be funnier than Eddie Murphy in *Raw*, and your own momma better be tight and right from head to toe! If both of these are on point, then you better know how to throw hands in a fight because depending how deep you go in on a person, somebody's feelings will get hurt and they will be ready to settle the score in the streets!

Can you guess what happened next? Yep, you guessed it. I got into a fight behind joking. I said a joke (about the mom); they didn't like it and they were waiting for me when we got off the bus. They—meaning a brother and sister—were ready to jump me. I mean seriously y'all, the joke wasn't even that funny and everybody was joking about mommas, so why it had to be different for me I will never know. Then again, yes, I do. I do know why and here's how I know.

I'm the oldest of my mother's children. I am also the oldest of all of the grandchildren born to my maternal grandparents. Although I had cousins who were close to my age, we didn't live around each other. After getting bullied in middle school, I wanted an older brother or sister who would take up for me and fight for me and prevent me from being picked on. I said it so much that it actually showed up on the day I needed it most: First Fight Day!

Where I lived on Indian River Road, there were two brothers who lived directly across the street. They were tough as nails and were not to be messed with. Everyone in the neighborhood knew who they were and feared them in a good way, unless you got on their bad side. Whoever got on their hit list back then tried their hardest to stay in hiding, but they couldn't hide forever. Just picture a thumb slowly gliding across the neck when they caught up to you. Yikes!

Back to the fight… I was the last one to get off the bus. I had never been in a fight before this one and had no clue what to do except swing my arms and fists like I saw other girls do at school. My heart was pounding in my chest so hard that you could see it beating through my shirt. My adrenaline was kicking in stronger and stronger with each step I took to the front of the bus. The bus driver looked at me like I was John Coffey walking *The Green Mile.* I was so tempted to ask if I could ride home with her, but I knew I would face the same problem the next day so might as well get it over with.

I stepped off the bus and the sister jumped in my face and said, *"Now what you say about my momma?"*

We were nose to nose, my knees were knocking, and I think I peed like two or three drops of pee, but I stood toe to toe, eye to eye, and replied, *"You heard me, I didn't stutter!"*

So now her brother starts walking towards me, cursing me out and instigating the sister to just, *"Smack the shit outta her, and beat her ass so we can go home."* At the same time my angels intervened, and the two "Deebo" looking brothers came around the corner and quickly sprang into action. All I knew is that the sister and I hit each other at the same time and before she could get another lick in, Deebo #1 grabbed her and pushed her so hard she flew into the briar bushes. I just knew a huge mob fight was about to start and someone would call the police, so I took off, but when I got to the corner, something told me to turn around. I saw Deebo#2 cuff the brother up by his shirt; he lifted him up in the air and head-butted him so hard that he crumpled into a heap! Knocked him clean out!

The last thing I heard before I took off running again was the Deebo brothers warn everyone never to put their hands on me or there would be hell to pay. I felt invincible as word quickly spread that I was their "little sister," but more than anything, I knew that God heard me and was paying attention to little old me; I knew in that moment that this was the beginning of me knowing He cared about the smallest things that mattered to me. I asked for a brother who would fight for me and take up for me and He gave me two. Unfortunately, one of the brothers was killed in the late '80s due to gun violence, but I am still close with the living brother to this day.

Naturally I was in a couple more fights after that, as that's what came with the territory. There were others that I should've been in, but those fights never happened—which is a good thing because all of the fights stemmed around jealousy and people go off the deep end when they are fueled with something stronger than anger. I was unaware of how cute and pretty I was because I dealt with low self-esteem, but others saw what I didn't even pay attention to and this made me stand out as a very pretty girl even more. This, of course, made some of the rougher chicks really want to do damage like cutting my face with a razor or stabbing me up. I steered clear of them because I didn't know how to fight with weapons yet, but I didn't escape them all.

One girl who was known for fighting wanted to fight me over a boy who wasn't thinking about either of our young, immature tails, but evidently the fight was supposed to prove to him who deserved to be his girl. He was from New York—a small-time dealer—and he was intriguing to say the least. I really, really liked this guy and everything about him. He was a little older, dressed like a rapper with all of the flyest sweatsuits and a fresh pair of sneakers almost daily. He walked with that Big Apple swag, kept money in each pocket, and was the first I had seen with gold fronts. He also had a real tall box fade like Kid from the movie *House Party*, which made him stand out even more. I was just starting to shed my nerdy ways and was ready for a boyfriend. He was new to the area, which made things perfect because nobody had claimed him, and I had a penchant for being the first to do things.

He used to walk past my house several times a day to go to the corner store and would say hi on his way back but never made a move. I figured maybe he needed a little push, so one day I stopped him and stepped up to him. I asked him the lamest question that popped up in my mind, but hey, it worked. The days following, we started kicking it as we called it back then. We would talk on my front porch for a couple hours until I had to go inside. His Queens accent made me tingle in my lady parts, and his full lips used to hypnotize me to the point of picturing myself licking the cherry-flavored Chapstick off them bad boys. That boy was fine as hell and he knew it too! I wanted him to kiss me so bad because to me this meant we were an item, and then he would be off limits. I was determined to make him my man so I could brag about it, especially because it was him. All the girls I hung around had boyfriends, and I was the only oddball who didn't and quite frankly I was over it.

People were noticing us talking, and then they started talking about us to others. Next thing you know, other females from other parts of the neighborhood started hanging around my area more often than usual. Word started to spread around about this dude from NY with the high-top fade and smelled like Egyptian Musk and Baby Powder oil mixed together. He loved the attention from them, which cut into the attention he was giving me. I had to think quickly so that I wouldn't lose him altogether, and that's when I started sneaking out of the house to hang out with him down the street. I was around 15 or 16 and I still had a curfew, a bedtime, and was certainly not allowed to date or have a boyfriend, much less invite them inside my house. I wanted to impress him with my bad girl ways so much that I was willing to risk whatever punishment came from my secret rendezvous.

It didn't work in my favor the way I thought it would, but it didn't stop me from still claiming our so-called relationship. He didn't claim me the way I assumed he would, and that made me look worse and weak. I guess he was whispering the same sweet nothings in them other broads' ears that he was telling me because the next thing I know word gets back to me that one of them wanted to scrap with me over him. I was already familiar with this girl and her reputation. I didn't think I would be able to beat her so I started carrying around a little knife that was small enough to hide in my purse so my mom wouldn't find it but big enough to do damage when needed. I wasn't all that skilled at using it, but I was gone learn on whatever day I did use it, I could tell you that much! It was just the way it was where I'm from: young girls carrying razors in their cheeks or under their tongues, or little switchblades that could fit in their bras. We weren't into guns yet, but this was the closest thing to it that was going to prove whatever point we wanted to make to whomever we needed to get it across to.

Anyway, back to the fight. I had just come home from church and I was walking to the corner store with my best friend. Some time had passed since I heard about her wanting to fight, but since she lived on the other side of the neighborhood the chances of us running into each other were actually slim to none. As a matter of fact, I believe my end (the Boondocks) and her end (Sumler Terrace) were beefing, so unless you were deep with a squad you didn't roll solo to the side you didn't live in or you already knew what was up if you got caught. All you could hope for is that you made it out not too badly hurt up; otherwise you were taking a trip to Sentara Norfolk General to get stitched up. Real talk!

So here we are walking to the store, laughing and carrying on and about a block away my senses kick in: the hair is standing up on the back of my neck, but I don't know why. We get closer to the store and I see a group of girls that stayed on the other side. The first thing I question is why were they all the way down here when they had to pass at least three stores before they got to the one where I was going. One girl who lived on my end saw us coming and quickly turned around. Then I saw another girl who I knew for sure hung with my nemesis peek around the corner then quickly duck back.

Then I see her. My adrenaline was kicking in 100 miles per hour; I'm sticking my hand in my pocket to pull out my Lil Helper, only to realize I left it in my purse at home. I had nothing. I felt so powerless because I could sense she had something, but I didn't know what it was. I turned and looked at my best friend and by the look on my face she knew what I was thinking and she said, "You better not run!" I had no choice but to face the music of having to fight her straight up no matter how ugly the tune was.

There is a sentence, this one sentence that females ALWAYS say when they're about to set it off, when there is nothing else to say and you really have no substantiated reason as to why you want to fight another female—well, the REAL reason is because of jealousy and envy, but you can't outright admit that or you will get clowned for being a hater, so you gotta say something else that always warrants and justifies a fight: "I heard you were talking about me." When you say those exact words, whether there is truth to it or not, the ears of those who hear it automatically assume it's true and the gloves come off at that point.

So, before I could answer and dispute what she supposedly heard, she started mumbling and because I couldn't hear her, I moved closer, but it was what she wanted because she was already planning on sneaking a hit in. She didn't even finish the sentence before she round housed me and hit me dead center in my eye socket with a padlock. I ain't talking about the little teeny one with the key you use to lock your bike up—no, this girl had a full on, heavy-duty combination lock, the kind that goes on school lockers! On one hand I should've been flattered that she felt she needed such a thing to fight me, but on the other hand, I could've lost an eye that day, behind a dude who wasn't even worth the price of costume jewelry.

It took a minute to collect my wits and get myself together, but I was so blinded that there was no way it would've been a fair fight, so I just ran home. As much as I watched cartoons, I finally experienced what Tom and Jerry, Sylvester the Cat and whoever else did when they used to get hit so hard, they saw stars and birds flying around their head at the same time. I saw every galaxy in the universe and all nine planets too! I had a very vivid imagination back then, and I just knew my eye was going to be hanging out of my head by the time I could look in a mirror. It's by the grace of God that no serious damage was done. I could've been permanently maimed over a temporary and emotional decision.

What did affect me the most was the embarrassment surrounding this incident. It was mid-summer, so a lot of people were outside and witnessed what happened. That wasn't the last time we saw each other. The groups we hung in had run-ins off and on as time passed, but I could never get her back personally like I wanted to. It caused a root of vindication to coil so deep around my heart that the plan of revenge I wanted to exact on her was so vicious it was scary. Although I had many chances to do it, something always held me back, which ultimately protected both of us.

> **Trap Root #3** - *anger and rage filling my heart, which created a temper so bad I reacted and responded negatively to situations quickly, never taking into consideration the ramifications of my actions or the damage it caused to others.*

Chapter 5

USE WHAT YOU GOT
TO GET WHAT YOU WANT

So many more things happened after the last incident I spoke of and not much of it significantly impacted my life, but it did impact my life, if you know what I mean. Crack cocaine was so prevalent in my neighborhood that it was becoming a mini war zone. There were gangs from New York that fought or had gun fights in New York who came to our state and then into our neighborhood to continue their beef there. There were shootouts with machine guns and Uzis. There were friends robbing other friends, guys setting each other up for the almighty dollar, and some of this even resulted in deaths.

All of that shaped the way I thought, but nothing could have prepared me for my parents splitting up. I didn't understand the issues at the time because I was a teenager and couldn't comprehend grown-up matters despite how grown I claimed to be. My dad left the house during a very prevalent time in my life when I needed him the most. You really don't pay much attention to your loved ones until their absence is felt and noticed. Because he was my first example of a real man, I began navigating towards that example when I started to entertain the idea of dating. I didn't deal with boys in my age group; I went for the older guys. If I am to be completely honest, I was talking to grown men twice my age, and I wasn't even legal to drive yet! (Sorry Mom)

Looking back at it now, I know this desire was due to me trying to fill the void of everything I needed and was missing. I was looking for a lover, a father, a confidant and a boyfriend all in one. I was always ahead of my time in the way that I thought, talked or perceived things and I didn't think or comprehend on a small level.

Everything had to be big, or more than I could handle, because there was an internal driving force that pushed me to overcompensate for the areas I lacked in. My self-esteem, self-worth, and self-respect were all in the toilet, but they always seemed to pique when someone complimented me or gassed my head up with a bunch of empty promises and caused my alter-ego of being bold and confident to rise to the occasion.

This spilled over into the type of dude I was interested in, which, at the time, were the main examples I had and saw day in and day out: glorified drug dealers. My environment portrayed and illuminated what appeared to be glamorous, never thinking about the flip side to the coin, in which that lifestyle ended in two ways—death or prison. When you're young, dumb and stupid you don't take any of this into consideration. You want what you want and will stop at nothing to get it, plain and simple.

By now I had allowed the internal hand that frequently pushed me to go above and beyond to rule and reign in my life, so much that as long as I had what it took to do what I wanted to do, I just did it. Sometimes it worked; others it didn't, but my confidence had grown quite a bit so if it didn't work the first time, I was going to keep at it until it did, and I won. I carried this mindset in almost everything I put my mind to, but the biggest task at hand was snagging me a Big Willie.

I didn't want the boy standing on the corner slinging small rocks. Nah, I wanted the kingpin! The one the judge gave football number type sentences to if they got caught.

I wanted the one with a big street reputation and the money to match.

I wanted the guy pushing the weight, not breaking the weight down into $10 and $20 bags.

I wanted the dude that took his girl on shopping sprees on Delancey Street then hit the outlets to shop some more on the way back home.

I wanted him to take me to the finest restaurants and show me off around town like I was a trophy wife that he was proud to call his own.

It was what I wanted more than anything, and I went hard in the paint to get it. However, they never wanted me back the way I wanted them, which was probably—no, not probably—it *was* a good thing because most of the girlfriends and wives that were in this seemingly envied position went through all types of hell. Side chicks turned into side families, then baby momma drama, domestic abuse, repeated infidelities… You name it, they dealt with it.

The money made them stay and accept the disrespect, humility and oftentimes broken hearts until they couldn't take it anymore and opted to leave their cushy life behind, or the guy left them first for the next hottest thing on his list only to repeat the same behavior.

I saw it time and time again, but it still didn't stop me from wanting the glitz and glamour that came with that lifestyle, afforded by massive stacks of cash. It was safe to say I was a glutton for punishment and had an affinity for finding things out the hard way, but that's what happens when you are a rebellious, head-strong teenager: you can't see the forest for the trees until you run headfirst into the tree trunk going 100 mph.

Who was I kidding to think these guys saw me as anything other than a quick roll in the hay? Yeah, my body was starting to fill out, and I was mentally maturing rapidly but not enough to be classified or viewed as a full-grown woman. That's who and what they wanted, someone who could bail them out when things went down in the streets, and the dealers had to handle it accordingly.

A woman who knew how to take care of house and home and hold them down through thick and thin.

A lady who played her part and position as a gangster's wife or woman and didn't fold when the pressure was applied.

A wife who didn't pack up and leave every time his indiscretions came to her attention. Instead, she attacked his pockets or safe with as much enthusiasm and vigor as he did his latest flings until she was satisfied with the damage she inflicted back. After all, all is fair in love and war, right?

No matter how much I allowed my imagination to run wild, I had to face reality when these love interests of mine shot down or rebuffed my advances. I had nothing to offer them except my body, and by this time, I was taught another hard knock lesson: use what you got to get what you want.

Things started to get pretty bad in my house because my parents were so angry with each other. I remember one time my father dropped off a check for groceries and my mom visibly looked upset after he left. She was sitting in the living room looking so mad that I could almost see the steam coming out of her. I asked her what was wrong, to which she closed her eyes and softly replied, "Nothing," and got up to leave as if she didn't want to fall apart in front of me.

I saw it sitting on the bookshelf, so when she left the room, I made a beeline for it to see what could've possibly pissed her off. When I looked at the amount of the check my eyes almost bugged out of my head. It was for $35! I still remember like it was yesterday and although I didn't know much about relationships and responsibilities, but one thing was for certain, two things for sure; $35 was not going to do anything for five children who stayed hungry 24/7.

I judged him for years afterwards and held on to resentment from that one incident, but when I became a mother and struggled several times over to feed my own children, it became clearer to me that maybe that was the best he could do at the time, or maybe that was all he had to his name. That helped me to forgive him and have compassion for other fathers that were in the same boat.

I remember staring at the check with an incredulous look on my face because all I could think about was what in the world could be bought with this little bit of money. It was only enough to buy bread, bologna and cheese—nothing else. I stormed out of the house, mad at the entire world because it seemed like there was always something happening beyond my control. This sparked a righteous indignation inside that, no matter what, I was going to find a way to fix issues and solve problems that were connected to me, so that I would never feel hopeless and helpless ever again.

No sooner had I settled on this thought than I ran into one of my homeboys. He always had some type of hustle going on and stayed having money. He was a big dreamer like me, and we used to talk about the different businesses he and I both wanted when we were in middle school. As a matter of fact, he is the first person I had a business partnership with. He would buy big quantities of candy and sold them while we were at school. He brought me in on the deal, showed me what to do, how much to charge, and at the end of the day I brought him his cut.

Fast forward a few years later to the point I'm referring to now; he had moved into selling dope and was doing quite well. He didn't have an interest in being a big-timer as he was more into legit businesses, but his approach was always to see if he could do it, how much he could make doing it, then move on to something else. Come to think of it, he was also the first person I knew to have more than one stream of income flowing. Everyone else either had a job in corporate America or was a street pharmacist if you catch my drift.

Anyway, he saw that I was noticeably upset and asked me what was wrong. I fought back tears while I told him what was going on, and he listened to me intently until I was done. I wasn't expecting sympathy from him, and I didn't ask him to financially help me out, but I sure as heck wasn't ready to be challenged so quickly in launching my fiery crusade of solving my problem either.

He squinched his eyes like he was asking a question through them. I asked what the look was for, and he said, "So are you going to cry about it or do something about it?"

I looked him in his eyes and said, "Whatever you got, let me in on it."

He said he needed somebody to push product in one of the local projects where his sister lived. He said nobody had truly claimed her corner and it was up for grabs. The plan was while she sold weed inside the house, she would watch me while I stood outside on the corner and we could get money both ways. Nothing sounds like a bad idea when you're hungry, your stomach is growling, and you can't even think about where your next meal is coming from because you haven't even eaten the first meal.

I told him I would do it, but I needed to make money right now to feed my brothers and sister and put groceries in the house. He gave me five small cellophane bags of crack cocaine worth $20.00 each and said, "Let me see what you can do with this; then I'll bring you out the way."

I wasn't scared or nervous about selling drugs because I had seen it done so many times, I could run my own small-time operation. I made runs or ran errands for other dealers to put a couple dollars in my pocket, so I knew what to do and how. Morally and ethically, I knew better, but all of the right and wrong way to do things went out the window because I was tired of seeing my mother struggle.

I was tired of not having money to do what I needed and wanted to do as a young teenager, which often left me out of many activities that required money to participate.

I was tired of not being able to dress the way I wanted to dress and buy the things I wanted to buy because all of the money had to go to bills.

Even so, my mother was very practical with the way she spent money, and there was no way she was going to spend over a certain amount, and certainly not for nobody's name-brand sneakers and clothes. All of my school clothes either came from Roses or some other type of low-end department store. When you get to a certain age, there is a certain status and appearance you want to maintain, so naturally, when you cannot hit this level, there is a growing frustration that pushes you and propels you towards getting what you need by any means necessary.

So here I am standing on the corner thinking I am about to make the quickest $100 I have ever made in my life. It was a no-brainer; I saw it time and time again and I could do it in my sleep. There were other teenagers my age and even younger walking around with thousands of dollars. Knots of money would make thick, square shapes in their pants. On certain days, sales would come in back to back so fast all they could do was stuff the money in their pockets and keep rolling.

Money was plentiful to the point where it was nothing to see bulging pockets on the young dudes and old heads, both of which were careless and had callous attitudes with the money they made. It was no big deal if a $50 or $100 bill fell out. They knew they could make it back within a matter of minutes, so the value of the almighty dollar was almost nonexistent.

But such was not the case for me. By this time, God had been showing up in different ways, in different situations, letting me know I was covered. Sometimes I could feel an unseen presence standing next to me and whatever problem I faced miraculously worked out in my favor. That didn't always mean a good thing, especially if I knew I was about to do something wrong. Those were the times I wanted Him to turn a blind eye, so I could do what I wanted with no interference.

This was one of those times when things didn't work out the way I had planned, and the quick fix to my problem remained a problem. What was supposed to be a few minutes of work turned into five hours, and I had only sold one $20 bag! I was frustrated, beyond mad and uber angry because my elaborate plan had completely failed. I thought to myself, *You have to be a special kind of loser to NOT be able to sell drugs!*

Let me explain the scenario so I can truly drive the point home: I lived in one of the most drug-infested areas in Norfolk. I knew who all of the addicts were and their drug of choice. Some preferred heroin, while others liked cocaine. Some wanted to sniff, others wanted to shoot up. Then you have those who either smoked crack or smoked weed; whatever floated their boat. I always knew who had what, so in case someone ran out, I could tell them where to go and who to see. Point is, I knew who they were and they certainly knew who I was.

My mom is going to freakin' kill me when she reads this, but it's the truth. I was in the worst spots, hanging with crooks and thinking nothing of it. Anything could've happened at any time, but I was completely oblivious to the obvious hand of protection that covered me. It was the norm for all of us youngsters to hang around the dope dealers and pushers and sometimes hang out in crack houses just shooting the breeze. It was the way of life for us, and we saw no harm in it.

Now back to my dilemma. With me describing and talking about this, clearly I'm not new to the scene. In other words, I was no stranger to these same people I saw day in and day out, but for some odd reason, NONE of them would buy from me! I had the look and the stance the corner boys had that let the whole world know they sold drugs. I mean the body language couldn't have been clearer, and I couldn't have looked more obvious, yet they walked right past me and went to someone else nearby.

I was standing there looking like a complete fool and was starting to grow desperate. At one point I even flashed my hand to show what I had. That was a rookie move, but I was aggravated and doing whatever came to mind.

If you're from the streets, then you know the name of the game is to act like you don't sell drugs, not announce it to the world! It was known that undercover police were setting up in houses to watch all the action, take photos and video footage to make stronger cases in court against those they had targeted, and here I am "volunteering as tribute" like the *Hunger Games*, just begging to be seen and caught! Like I said, I was a special kind of loser.

When my homeboy left me earlier, he went to check on his other spots to collect money and sell more weight to the guys who bought product from him. He thought I was agitated because a few hours had passed, and he naturally assumed I had been waiting on him because I had probably sold what I had hours ago.

Ignoring my angry facial expression, he flashed his pearly white teeth with a shiny gold tooth on the side and said, "What you got for me?" Silently I opened my hand and his smile disappeared. He looked at me in disbelief and said, "Damn girl, whatchu been out here doing all this time? Running yo mouth?"

I lied and told him the addicts said the crack rocks were too small, and they went to other people to be serviced. He told me not to trip, said we should just head out to Roberts Park so I could post up at his sister's house. Roberts Village—affectionately known as "the park"—was a project housing area off of Princess Anne Road and Ballentine Boulevard in Norfolk, VA.

This was one of those areas where if you weren't from there, you best not to come there! The drug game was bringing out the savagery in the most unlikely people, simply because the potential to make as much money as you wanted was breeding jealousy and envy in those who weren't making as much or who were just plain greedy and wanted to take what you worked hard to build.

On the way to his sister's house, we talked about what was going on in my life and what I planned on doing with the money. My whole goal was to help my mom pay bills, but I had big dreams that would require big money. I wanted to get my own hustle going to afford what I saw dancing around in my mind.

I wanted to live a lavish life like the girlfriends of the guys I hung around, but I also wanted to make money like they did and become a "Queenpin". I figured if they could do it, then so could I. I saw what my mom was dealing with, going from a homemaker to now having to work two jobs, and that still wasn't enough. I hated seeing the sadness in her eyes from dealing with the effects of divorce during the day and hearing her cry herself to sleep at night.

He got really quiet and I asked what was on his mind. He said, "Queta, this life that you want, it ain't for you. I hear you, but I also know you. I know your heart and you're too nice to be grimy. You can't be soft or these dudes will run up on you and take everything you got, including your life! I just don't wanna see you get hurt like that, baby girl."

I looked at him intently and nodded in agreement, but the look in my eyes spoke another language. I thought quietly to myself that I would just take my chances and figure out the rest if it ever came down to it. I had a cute face and thought that would sway someone from running up on me.

Well, what do you think happened next? Yeah, someone tried

me. Well, they tried to try me, but my angelic help showed up in the nick of time.

When my homeboy dropped me off at his sister's house, I talked to her for a little while to hear what the plan was. She told me she would watch from the window and if anything looked shaky, she would shoot first and ask questions later. I said "Aight … bet," and went outside.

I had way better progress when I hit the corner. Not only did I sell everything I went out there with, but I was also moving on to the other "package" he had inside the house. That's when I kept noticing a couple of dudes eyeing me but really didn't think anything of it. I figured they were trying to figure out who the cutie with the bootie was and would eventually make their way over to try to holla at me.

Little did I know, they had been watching my moves and were plotting to rob me. As I said earlier, nobody had that particular spot as of yet, but apparently they were going to move in on it, until we showed up. Just as I thought, they came over and asked if I had a boyfriend and where was I from because they hadn't seen me out there before, etc.

I gave short answers because I was trying to be low-key and talk to them at the same time. I started feeling uneasy and noticed one of them kept easing behind me inch by inch, which caused my hairs to stand up on my neck. The tone of the conversation shifted from them talking nice to now talking a little gruff.

They said more than once, "Shorty, you must not know where you at or you would've come out here strapped." I felt my warning antennas go off and immediately started looking towards the window. I didn't see sis posted up, so I had to think quickly.

I remembered hearing the older guys say you always look your opponent or enemy in the eyes; don't show fear and don't back down. I was shaking like a leaf, scared as hell, but I refused to go out like a sucka, so I looked at both of them and said, "I ain't gotta go nowhere strapped! My brother Crazy Eddie will be out here real soon to pick me up, and when he does, y'all be sure to stick around so I can tell him what y'all said!"

The look on both Dumb's and Stupid's face was priceless. I mentioned the name of someone who was a straight menace to society, someone who played no games and grew a reputation for his public displays of handling what he perceived as problems. He was from New York but was notoriously known in the Hampton Roads area. I don't know what it was, but I had a penchant for hanging with guys like this, so it was nothing to have a car full of goons pull up and let their presence be known in the worst way.

By this time, sis was coming out the front door with a gun in her hand. She asked them what the problem was and did it need to be solved. They were still white in the face behind the name I mentioned, so when they saw the gun they needed no further coaxing to hightail it. She told me she was handling a customer in the back and when she came to the window she stopped because she wanted to see how I was going to handle myself.

She turned philosophical on me said, "The game is gritty and you gotta be ready at all times, for whatever to happen at all times. These guys don't care if you're a female or not, all they see is money and if something or someone is standing in the way of them getting it, then that person or thing has gotta go … simple as that!"

I listened intently and at that moment I made up my mind that this wasn't the life for me and I needed to quit while I was ahead. I had already lost a few friends behind the drug game, and it hurt like hell to know I would never see them again behind a temporary high or money that was going to be spent just as quickly as it came. Sometimes you gotta know when to fold your hand and walk away. This was for sure one of those times and I didn't need to think twice about it either.

After my near-robbery experience, I felt so lost and out of place that I started being reckless with my actions. I was developing a terrible temper from all of the anger and rage stemming from everything that was going on or had previously happened and because I didn't know how to channel it, it was putting me in some bad situations.

I was dealing with rejection, feeling like an outcast and totally misunderstood. All I wanted was this great life I had constantly dreamed of; it seemed attainable, but the more I strived for it the more it eluded me. I would get so close to grasping it; then it would slip through my fingers like smoke from an apparition. I felt like I was sounding like a broken record to those closest to me. They had helped me to come up with solutions, but nothing seemed to go as planned, and that frustrated me more. I wanted to keep asking and probing them for more answers, but their frustration grew right along with mine, not because they didn't want to help me, but they had their own issues to deal with. It was when the well of others' suggestions started to dry up that I started to shut down.

When I look back on it, God was using those moments to drive me towards Him. He wanted me to remember how I used to talk to Him and include Him in everything that mattered to me, but as all of His children do from time to time, I strayed and fell out of the practice that used to bring me peace. One of the many things that I love most about God is that He uses all things to accomplish the one thing that matters to Him the most: fellowship with His daughters and sons, and He knew it was only a matter of time before I remembered where I left Him standing and would reunite with Him and fall back in step with Him on this life's journey.

He brought to my remembrance a park my mother used to take us to when we were younger with a huge lake in the middle of it. I remember sitting close to it, closing my eyes and having the deepest talks with God there. I would leave feeling like I was vibrating on the highest frequency I could and feeling so empowered. There is something about water that causes me to open up and to surrender to the serenity that ebbs and flows from the movement of the current. I couldn't believe that I had forgotten about this sacred place and quickly figured out a way to get there.

Lakeside Park in Chesapeake, VA is where families had reunions, cookouts, and birthdays and anything else worth celebrating. It was whatever anyone needed that location to be, but it meant more to me as this was a place where I knew God met me, sat with me and conversed with me. I felt a tug and a pull to get there, so I called one of my homeboys who had a car and got him to take me. Going to "the spot" became a thing we did often as it calmed his spirit too. He always commented on how deeply I thought and talked and marveled at the things I verbally expressed. He admired how different I was and said I was a breath of fresh air, especially since we could have friendly banter about intellectual things he stated other girls my age weren't even talking about, much less thought, or were afraid to discuss as they were seen as taboo subjects.

All I needed was for someone to listen to me, allow me to really express myself and help me sort things out, or just sit quietly while we watched the water and I silently prayed. *Lord, I really need answers and I need a change. If you don't help me, no one else will and I don't think I'm gonna make it.* I cherish those times because I honestly believe I would've lost it if I didn't have that as an outlet. Just when I thought my prayers went unanswered or were swallowed up by the lake, heaven smiled upon me.

Chapter 6

CONCRETE JUNGLE WHERE DREAMS ARE MADE OF

God has a way of showing up at the times we need Him the most and that ray of sunshine always got me through. He answered my prayer by the lake and presented an opportunity for me to leave VA for a while. I spent the summer of 1991 in New York with my uncle, who was a celebrity hair stylist. I worked at Bumble and Bumble in Manhattan on 7th and 56th. He lived in a penthouse on 7th and 54th and I felt like I hit the jackpot! I needed to see something different outside of the chaos and mayhem I was used to seeing on a daily basis and this was the very world-changing view I needed in the nick of time!

Like every other New Yorker who walked to work, I loved the hustle and bustle and the large crowds of people walking with purpose. They all walked swiftly like they had people to see, places to be and things to do. No time to fool around, everyone was on their money grind. It sparked something familiar in me, as making moves was embedded in me: Norfolk raised me, but Berkley made me, and I was taught by the best to get it from the mud and build a palace with it!

I walked past designer stores every day, window shopping and dreaming of the day I would buy shoes from Ferragamo or pants from Fendi. I even swore I would only wear makeup from Chanel and dresses from Gucci. I was tall and slender with a body that could wear anything, so I decided I would move back and pursue a career as a dancer and a model.

At that time Donald Trump was one of my favorite people in the world and I considered it a privilege and an honor to walk past Trump Tower. The wealth and richness that walked through those evolving doors was breathtaking. You could literally smell the money oozing from there.

I made the doorman laugh every day with a knock-knock joke or something else funny to say while I stopped at the bagel and coffee bodega and ordered my usual; everything bagel with cream cheese or lox, with light roasted coffee and tons of cream and sugar.

Bumble and Bumble was a salon like no other. I worked as a shampoo girl at Hair Doctor's on 21st Street for a guy named Calvin from DC. I could shampoo the heck outta some hair and received many compliments on how gifted my hands were. I knew what to do, but nothing prepared me for the upscale level-up when I walked in this salon. My uncle was the stylist for Madonna, Michael J. Fox, Melba Moore and many others. Once again, the wealth that sat in the seats getting pampered was overwhelming. I looked at the final bill for one lady and it was around $525! I almost keeled over because I could never fathom anyone paying that much for anything—let alone hair!

I was 17 at the time and I wasn't quite used to big purchases like that, but the more I saw it the more I wanted it to be my life as well and I was completely sold on New York being my new home when I graduated from school. I was going to work in the salon while looking for anything dealing with the arts. I loved to dance and had some experience in acting, and since New York was the concrete jungle where dreams were made of, surely my big break was about to crack the sky open looking for me. I had everything mapped out, which made me even more amped to graduate from high school, but as usual life would show up with something else to derail me, as if it were intent on destroying me atom by atom until I disintegrated.

Chapter 7

UNCLE SAM AND HIS MINIONS

It seemed as if I was chasing every glimmer of light that looked like a turning point in my life. I desperately wanted normalcy; I yearned for good things to happen to me more than the bad that had, but just life was making a turn for the better, it took a turn for the worse. My cousin, who's slightly younger than me, was shot in the face with a sawed-off shotgun and it maimed him so badly he stayed in the hospital for months. It's by the grace of God he survived something so horrific, especially enduring the pain of reconstructive surgeries and the healing process. A few years before that happened, my aunt, Janet Mabine Jenkins, was working the night shift at a convenience store in Ahoskie, NC and was stabbed to death by two guys trying to rob the place. Not only did this rock our family to the core but the community as well as those types of violent acts didn't really occur in that area.

My relationship with my mother was not on the best of terms because of my rebellion and being a typical teenager times ten. She had already put me out a couple of times to go stay with other family members until I could get my act together then allowed me to come home, but not without more of my antics. I was so over life itself and things happening to people that I cared about and truly loved that I started to really act up. I was skipping school, barely did schoolwork when I did attend, and slept through classes all the other times. I was depressed, withdrawn and couldn't have cared less about anything at that point.

When I was 19, I decided to go into the military. My life was on a downward spiral, but thanks be to God I had enough sense to do something about my situation before it was too late. I initially wanted to join the Air Force, but because I had a one-year-old son, they wouldn't allow me to. He needed to be adopted, which normally takes a couple of years. I didn't have that kind of time, so the Army was glad to shuffle me over to their office. They allowed me to give legal guardianship to my mother, which only takes a day to complete. I started the process thinking I was going to leave in a matter of months, only to be placed on their deferment list for a year.

As I look back, I realize this was a plot and trick of the enemy to get me trapped so I wouldn't break out of the molded environment I was in. I grew up and lived in a neighborhood filled with drug dealers, drug addicts, hustlers and everything else in between and when you're exposed to this and see it daily, you can't help but pick up bad habits through osmosis. You start to evolve with the environment and don't even realize it. This is the path I embarked upon and after a few incidents and brushes with death, I knew I had to do something to get away or I wasn't going to live much longer. I did my best to stay out of trouble and keep my nose clean so I could leave on my intended date. Any mishaps with the law would alter all my plans and I would've been stuck in a matrix designed to destroy me. Finally, the day came for me to start a new life and on November 3rd, 1993 I left the old and embraced the new.

I did basic training in Fort Jackson, SC in the brutal cold. Back then, you could tell the seasons apart and there were no sunny, warm days around Thanksgiving and Christmas like there are now. We had a holiday break, so instead of being finished in the normal eight weeks, we didn't graduate until February 4, 1994. My next assignment was in Fort Gordon, GA where I studied to become a telecommunications specialist. I scored very high on the ASVAB test and this was the best job they had. It required me to have a top security clearance, which set me apart from my peers. I remember a drill sergeant telling me that I stuck out like a sore thumb. I looked at him with a mean look, thinking he was being the ogre we knew him to be during basic training, but he clarified it after he saw my facial expression. He said, "No matter what you do, there is a light about you that you cannot hide. You're different from others and for that reason alone, you will go far in life." He said he saw great things in me and expected me to succeed in my military plans and career goals.

After five months of AIT (Advanced Individual Training), I learned of my first duty station: Fort Clayton, Panama! I was in shock because I just knew I would have what was on my dream sheet of duty stations I desired, but overseas was NOWHERE on my list! When you sign up to serve your country, however, you go where you are needed—point blank, no questions asked! I left the states in June of 1994 and entered one of the hottest places I ever experienced. My mother's family is from Ahoskie, NC and if you know anything about the heat in the South, you know that's about as close as you get to feeling how hot Hell is!

So here I am, the new kid on the block, or a "newbie" as we were jokingly called. I walked with confidence, I exuded intelligence and I had my head screwed on straight. My body was so fit and muscled from all of the physical training that I turned the heads of men and women, which sometimes brought a lot of unwanted attention. Immediately men in higher ranks started to approach me, but I turned them down with finesse. I had dreams and goals I wanted to accomplish on my own and not by sleeping my way to the top.

They kept trying and I kept dodging, until one day I was cornered. I lived in the barracks, which was unisex, but our roommates were the same gender. I had just gotten out of the shower when there was a knock on my door. One of the lieutenants came looking for my roommate supposedly, but it was a ruse to come on to me. When an officer of rank comes in your presence, you're supposed to address them by saluting and give respect no matter how awkward the situation may be.

Here I am half-dressed, waiting for this dude to finish with the dumb questions that I knew were just his way of phishing and trying to feel me out, but I wasn't budging. He made a feeble attempt to pull rank on me and said that he could make my life easy or hard, the choice was mine. I asked what the hell that was supposed to mean. At this point, the street ways in me were coming out; I knew what he was implying, so now I was in defense mode, ready for a word-for-word showdown. If he could disrespect me by giving me a sexual ultimatum, then I was going to disrespect him with my answers. At this time my roommate came in and startled him, so he mumbled something and quickly walked out. I told her what happened, and she warned me that he "always does this to the new girls" and to be careful.

Months went by and every now and again I would see the lieutenant. He would smirk at me and I would grit on him and roll my eyes. Word was that he was being transferred to another base, so I did my best to avoid him until he left. I thought I was good until one night my luck ran out. A few of my Army buddies and I had come back from hanging out at the NCO club, a hangout spot that was on the base. I was a bit drunk, but not to the point where I was wasted. He was on duty that night and probably watched us from one of the windows spilling out of the cab, making a bunch of noise, and bidding each other good night.

I'm sure he saw when I went in my room because his timing was a little too perfect. He knew my roommate was on leave, which meant I was alone. I had just undressed and slid in my bed when he used the master key to come in and had his way with me. When he finished, he said if I told anyone, it would be his word against mine. He continued on to say he could mess my records up so that I wouldn't advance or, worse yet, get me put out of the military with a dishonorable discharge. I didn't know any better, so I believed him. I was in the process of studying for tests and doing what I needed to do to advance and didn't need any setbacks.

I thought it was a dream until I told one of my girlfriends the next day what had happened, and her response was, "Oh, he got you too?" I was in such shock; I just cried uncontrollably because up to that point I thought I was dreaming.

The day came when his tour ended and he was being sent to another duty station, undoubtedly to take advantage of someone else. I started feeling at ease and wasn't feeling anxious all the time, which allowed me to return to being my normal self. A year passed by and I resumed going after my next military goals with vigor. I rekindled my relationship with the guy I was seeing and all seemed to be right in my life. I was in a better head space; I started healing mentally and emotionally and was starting to feel better about life until it happened again. My platoon deployed to Suriname,

South America for training and to oversee the Cubans fleeing the communistic regime of Fidel Castro.

I was walking back from my rounds, making sure our communication equipment was intact, when the company sergeant major pulled me into his tent. He was a big, burly guy—sort of reminded you of an ogre with his hairy body and menacing appearance. Apparently, he had been drinking because he reeked of alcohol. He asked me about the checkpoints and if the guard shacks were secure. His words slurred so badly that I could barely make out what he was saying. I started to feel nervous and uneasy so told him I would give him a report the next day. When I turned to leave, he grabbed me by my arm and said he hadn't dismissed me yet.

He started fondling me roughly, telling me how much I had turned him on since I had arrived at the unit and whatever else he could think of. He made me touch his genitals, forcing me to rub him until he became fully erect, and then tried to push my head down to perform oral sex. There was no way in hell I was going to put my mouth on that sweaty, nasty stub! This time I was going to fight back, and I didn't give a damn what the aftermath was. I tried to scream and push him off, but he was strong as hell, I mean ridiculously strong! I was hoping someone was going to hear the scuffling and come barging in, but we were surrounded by noise, so my cries went unheard.

Some kind of way he had my arms folded up in a pretzel position. As many times as I had successfully gotten out of this hold during my self-defense training, my mind went blank. I think it was the position I was in that when I moved, excruciating pain shot through my body and sort of disabled me. He managed to pull my shorts down and penetrated me. It was over in a matter of seconds because Shrek had no type of penal control. He got one pump in and was done. Thank God for erectile dysfunction in this case!

He released himself on the dirt floor and my arms right after. He kicked dirt over the semen and dug it in the ground as if he was getting rid of anything to incriminate him. He told me to get myself together before I left and walked away as if nothing happened. The cockiness, the gall and the audacity he displayed assured me that he had done this many times before, which is why he had zero problems with my attempts to be heard and rescued. He was so damn ugly, and he knew this, which is why he took what he wanted. He was overly confident that he would get away with it due to his rank, status and superior relationships in high places.

I was in such a daze walking back to my tent, wondering how this happened to me again, but this time was worse than the last because of the action that took place. I felt so violated, so yucky inside and no matter how much I showered, I wasn't clean enough. Every time it replayed in my mind, I vomited. I couldn't eat, didn't do any of my duties and only left my tent to use the bathroom. I got so sick and dehydrated I had to be med-evacuated to the unit back in Panama. Before the helicopter touched the landing pad, I had made up in my mind that I wasn't going to take an "L" on this one.

I hunted down the captain of my unit and told him what happened, sparing no detail. He looked shocked and distraught while listening to me, but when I told him that it had happened before with the lieutenant, to me and a couple other girls, it was like he had been gut-punched. It took everything in him to fight his tears and not break down in front of me. Reason being, he was responsible for us as soldiers in his unit, especially the females, and his job was to protect us at all costs. I think he was angrier that these incidents were happening under his command yet he was clueless and didn't know that his own peers were the culprits.

My commander took a special interest in me when he recognized the hunger I had to excel, along with the drive and focus needed to go far. He took me under his wing and started mentoring me. Not that he wouldn't do this for anyone, but a certain group of us had the "wow factor" as he called it and he wanted to have a personal hand in helping us succeed in our military careers. We were also great friends; I grew to trust him and his judgment, which up to that point was sound and wise. He viewed me like a little sister, so it hurt him that I was hurt like that. The other reason for his anguish was the dilemma he was facing because he was also friends with the sergeant major. They were very close as they had served in a war together, so this put him in a serious predicament. He told me he would deal with it but asked me to give him time to figure things out. He told me to keep it to myself for now, and when they got back from deployment, he would see to it that I received justice.

Well, that never happened. I expected my commander to do his civic duty to me as a member of the armed forces, a soldier in the Army, and a vital member of the 534th MP Unit. This should have been top priority as opposed to saving face and salvaging his friendship, but obviously it must have been too complicated for him to handle. His temporary solution was to offer for me to report for duty at another location so I could avoid seeing the sergeant major, but that was like putting a Band-Aid on a stab wound. I wanted to see this man brought up on charges, lose all of his rank, get demoted to the lowest position on the chart and possibly jail time. If I had things my way, I would've handled it myself because I was ballsy like that, but I couldn't do it because I didn't have the juice to demand meetings with people who sat in high places. And even if I could, guess who the damn paperwork had to go through for approval since everything in the military had to "follow the chain of command"? You got it—the ogre himself!

Once I saw that I was being given the runaround, I started to feel like I didn't matter, that my life didn't mean shit to the Army outside of me doing my part by serving my country and keeping their numbers right. I was replaceable and what happened to me was an "Oh well, suck it up soldier, and deal with it" situation. All of my plans, dreams and goals went up in smoke right before my eyes and I grew hateful towards the military and everything it stood for.

I prayed and asked God to give me a way out as my thoughts were starting to become irrational and all over the place. My relationship with the guy I was seeing was in shambles by this time, yet I held on to what was left. He could tell something was wrong, but every time I brought myself to tell him about the incident, I clammed up. I felt so ugly and viewed myself as a worthless piece of trash. I would physically feel sick when I attempted to talk, and in my mind, I thought he would think the worst of me. I couldn't take another bad thing happening to me, so I clammed up and left it alone.

My appetite for sex with him became insatiable, but it also posed a problem. It was all I wanted and that was so unlike me. I used to be outgoing, fun to be around, joked a lot, laughed hard and loved even harder. I was affectionate and used to look forward to cuddling in silence, only hearing his heartbeat. That's who he fell in love with. We went from being close friends to only getting together when I wanted him to love my body, to love the emptiness away, and nothing more. We grew distant but not before he left a major part of himself with me.

A short time after we grew apart, I found out I was pregnant. To me this was the sign I needed that my prayer had been answered. My contract was for four years with no room to breech it, unless there was a dire reason the government deemed worthy of accepting. Other than that, your ass was grass, and you belonged to Uncle Sam and his minions until they used you up and threw you away. There were special circumstances such as pregnancy, issues with being overweight, or serious medical conditions that hindered you from "being all you can be in the Army." All warranted quick releases and thankfully with an honorable discharge.

My commander tried his best to talk me out of it, but I was adamant about sticking to my decision. He didn't understand that I could feel that I had changed drastically and I could not take a chance with whatever actions might stem from something making me angry. One time I had seen the sergeant major from a distance and my heart was pounding so hard I could feel it beating through my BDU jacket. I started sweating and could feel the heat rising up in me from the rage brewing inside. That's when I knew I needed to put some major distance between me and him, otherwise I would probably still be in Ft. Leavenworth to this day for committing a gruesome crime.

I gave up quite a few of the benefits that I had either built up on my own or were afforded to me. It wasn't until a couple years later that I learned just how much I had forfeited and how that one decision to save my life cost me more than the average person would've lost in five lifetimes.

Chapter 8

THE STRUGGLE WAS BEYOND REAL

The silver lining to me chucking up the deuces to what seemed like a toxic relationship with the Army was that I left in good standing and I could breathe without feeling like a plastic bag was over my head. The downside is that it was the beginning of a nightmare, the kind in which you die all types of horrible deaths over and over, and no matter what you do, you never fully wake up. It was also the beginning of me displaying symptoms and tendencies that stemmed from a syndrome a lot of ex-military members were dealing with but had no face and no name.

When I first got home, I was questioned constantly by my family and friends as to why I got out because, to their understanding, I was going to be gone for a while. They had seen me a couple times on leave, but they were prepared not to see me for few years based on the content of my letters and extensive conversations via long-distance phone calls. I didn't know what to say, I had no other valid reason that made sense outside of my pregnancy, and I certainly didn't want to rehash the truth because I knew they would ask a thousand questions and I didn't want to deal with the way it made me feel. I had already begun the process of blocking out what happened as it became the best way to deal with life, but it came with a price as it suppressed my ability to be emotionally connected.

Let me shift gears here for a moment and explain some things a bit deeper. Around 1997 was when my personal issues began to really need some attention, but I didn't start doing research until 2012 on what was wrong and how it could be fixed. I was officially released from active duty in December 1996, but it took a couple of years before what I had suppressed and blocked out began to manifest. The syndrome that a lot of veterans and military members were dealing with but had no name for is PTSD (Post Traumatic Stress Disorder). This is caused by anything traumatically seen or experienced; whether it is from the collateral damage of war, or issues within the armed forces, this is typically how a soldier is affected with this syndrome.

However, this didn't occur until many years later and after I suffered and struggled in the areas mentioned. From 1995 to 2013 I was clueless that I even had this issue-turned-disability, which meant it went untreated all those years and I grew worse. Back then, there wasn't a title, nor was it even recognized, but many were suffering from it. It wasn't until different people with the same allegations and the same issues were coming forward in droves that the government was forced to take a look into these claims and not sweep them under the rug like they did everything else that would stain or tarnish the armed forces' precious reputation.

I feel the need to explain something here. So many people think this is a "military term" and that couldn't be further from the truth. PTSD does not happen to just military personnel; it can affect civilians too. Think about tragic or horrific accidents, domestic situations, violence, etc. All of these occurrences can have negative impacts on those that witness these atrocities, for everyone's ability to deal with trauma is different. It doesn't make you weaker than the next person because of your inability to handle it a certain way, but it can eventually weaken you mentally if you don't seek help. Think about what has taken place in America, your family, and things that happened around you that were out of your control. Life just inserts whatever it wants at any given moment, but how you handle a thing is how you overcome it. No one is exempt from unforeseen situations happening to them, and if people understood the difficulty of being an involuntary victim, there would be less ridicule and more empathy.

PTSD can cause you to live in constant fear, anxiety and stress. It becomes the unwanted houseguest overstaying its welcome, infringing itself upon your daily lifestyle and schedule, and no matter what you do to get rid of it, it pops up at the most inopportune times without remorse.

PTSD symptoms prevalently show in your choices and actions; you feel like a marionette puppet being pulled by strings to do things that under normal circumstances you wouldn't do. What seems right is typically wrong, and common-sense stuff seems too good to be true, so you shy away and leave things unattended rather than deal with them.

You can be in a room full of people and still feel alone or become so much of an introvert that you cut off communication with those who love you and care about you. Eventually you allow relationships to fall to the wayside simply because you feel like your issues are too burdensome for others to bear. Paranoia becomes the norm; isolation becomes a blanket of comfort and depression becomes the garment you wear on a daily basis.

After I had my daughter in 1996, I had four more children afterwards. I honestly believe that post-partum depression not only triggered the PTSD but added to it. I should've been clinically depressed after having all of these children, along with two miscarriages. I had my third child in 1998, my fourth in 2003, fifth in 2009 and my sixth and last in 2010. It is ONLY by the grace of God that I was not worse off!

Throughout the years I have witnessed many other women who had major issues with post-partem and unfortunately took their own lives. I cannot express enough how I KNOW God has preserved me for whatever reasons, because technically … scientifically … I should NOT be alive today! The one thing I will never do is take credit from the only ONE who kept me sane enough not to harm myself, my children or anyone else. Not only did He cover me, but He protected my children while in my womb and shielded them from ailments and issues they should've been born with.

Can you imagine the shame, the ridicule and the looks of disgust I received from people during those years? Or how I was being judged for my sporadic actions because they had become my norm? It was easier to talk about me and walk away from me so they wouldn't have to deal with me. No, I wasn't acting like someone who needed to be committed into an insane asylum. Thank God it wasn't that bad! But I was an emotional wreck, and an emotional person is just as dangerous as someone who is certified with papers. They base decisions off of emotions and that is never good. How do you think so many stories end up on *Lifetime*?

Emotions are fickle and change like the weather, and anyone who doesn't have a lid on them normally ends up in hot water. I still had a problem with my temper, which created a detrimental combo. This is what made friends and family look at me sideways; they never knew what mood I was going to be in and what actions would follow. I didn't go around starting problems or picking fights, but no one wants to deal with someone who can go from 0 to 100 in a matter of seconds if someone makes them mad or hurt their feelings. Anything could cap off and that places innocent people in precarious situations.

Nothing was easy during this time for me, and I looked for an outlet of comfort to ease the pain of what plagued me day in and day out. Drugs and alcohol were the most popular coping mechanisms but not limited to the list of vices people chose for comfort, which exceeded those two things. I had smoked weed a few times when I was younger, but since I was never a druggie type person, alcohol became my drug of choice. It became my weakness, my crutch, and the very arms I needed to embrace every part of me without judgment. I drowned my sorrows in liquor and cried myself to sleep with wine-induced tears saturating my pillows. This is how I coped and every chance I could get, I drank.

No one knew the reason behind my rage, so they didn't understand me. Hell, I didn't even understand me half the time! I didn't know how to articulate how I felt without falling apart at the seams or feeling like they were going to disown me because of how deep my problems ran. It wasn't until I started therapy and going through my own self-guided healing process that the root causes of issues begin to unravel. This brought enlightenment through understanding the why and the what, and once I had understanding I was able to really break free.

Chapter 9

I WAS BUILT FORD TOUGH FOR THIS

There is something about the oldest child that carries a lot of weight. They carry an inherent title of a "born leader" and it is presumed that they will accept this role with no questions asked. They are also considered curse-breakers or carry an anointing for breakthrough and deliverance in order for a family to shift from being broken and barren to wealthy and plentiful. They go through more issues and suffer greatly as they have to carry burdens not meant for feeble shoulders to bear alone, but God is always with them, covering them, protecting them and providing for them.

He protected me and shielded me from what should have completely and utterly destroyed me from a myriad of compounded difficulties. On one extreme, I was like a magnet for all things problematic and on the other end stability, consistency and normalcy eluded me like a high-speed chase. No matter how close I came to grabbing ahold of these dire needs, they seemed to slip through my grasp and dissipate into thin air.

My children were subjected to anything and everything I was dealing with, and what was meant to shape their lives negatively made them resilient, but I couldn't see it at the time. You would think that if this was my cross to bear then no one else should be affected by the hand that was dealt to me. Such was not the case for my children as they felt the brunt of all that I endured.

I couldn't get stable to save my life and that depressed me even more. We moved so many times, I don't think there was an address I didn't put my stamp on. We even had to stay in quite a few shelters from time to time if I was completely tapped out of funds. I thought I was the worst mom on the planet during those times. This was not the life I had imagined for my kids, but I did the best I could with what I had and with what I knew. If I didn't know anything else, I knew how to survive and if this was going to be my lot in life, I was going solicit the help of the government in every way possible since I was in this mess because of their negligence.

I heavily relied on government assistance, researching every program until I had them down to a science. After each child was born, I used WIC (Women Infants and Children) to cover their formula, milk and other nutritious food items necessary for their brain development and growth, until they were five years old.

I received food stamps, which fed us really well, but I would run out of food by that last week of the month. I supplemented this need by hitting as many food banks as possible that were within my radius. Most of them only allowed you to come monthly, which worked perfectly for me because that's when I would need them again. My grandmother taught me how to cook really well when I was 16, and being from the North Carolina, most of the meals were from scratch and were full course: a meat, vegetable and a side with dessert. I had to get creative in the last week, my "stretch week." Whatever came in the box of random stuff is what I threw together. I jazzed it up so well with herbs and seasoning that it looked good and tasted even better. I taught my kids to be grateful for what we had because some of their classmates didn't have anything to eat when they got home from school, much less a hot meal, and/or had parents that couldn't care less about their child's well-being and left them to fend for themselves.

My work ethic is through the roof, something I am proud to say I inherited from my grandparents. I never ever had an issue with getting a job, but *keeping* it proved to be the challenge. This made me extremely frustrated because I was working jobs that I was overqualified for, but since I lacked collegiate education and didn't have years behind the skills I had, I stayed underemployed, which meant underpaid. This forced me to choose which bills would get paid and what had to wait. I was tired of robbing Peter to pay Paul, but when you're stuck like Chuck, you don't have a choice but to stay on the hamster wheel.

When I was in between jobs, I had to learn how to work the system just to stay afloat with rent and utilities, but when the agencies ran out of funds, so did my instant help. When my kids were younger, we played hide and go seek in the dark when the lights were off. They were so happy and thought Mommy was being silly as they ran throughout the house until they tired themselves out. While they slept with a smile on their faces, I cried silently while figuring out what I needed to do.

My water was turned off a couple of times too, but we still had work and school to get to. I bought jugs of water to heat up so that we could wash up, brush our teeth and leave out the door as presentable as possible. While they were learning, I was hustling on my breaks, calling every agency that offered financial assistance until I had enough pledges to get the water turned back on before we came home.

But when it got to the point of me stealing gas from a gas station just to make it through the week, that's when I said enough is enough. I was nobody's thief and to have to stoop to that level of thievery made me feel like I had hit rock bottom. I had revisited the idea of working for myself, and the only person who could do something to change this narrative was me. I guess in a sense it was always in the cards for me due to more of life's challenges looming on the horizon.

I am most grateful that I didn't have sickly children who needed frequent doctor or hospital visits, but Israel, my youngest, went through all of the medical drama in place of his siblings. He was born with certain special needs that could've been avoided. When I was in labor with him, his oxygen levels dropped and went undetected for a while. If I was being monitored properly by the hospital staff (plight of black women and pregnancy) then I believe this would have been caught in time and he would not have been born with a developmental delay.

He was also born with a large growth on his tongue, and as he grew, so did this knot and it caused his tongue to protrude out of his mouth. I had to take him to an ENT specialist while in his infancy stages, and the term I was given was Lymphatic Malformation of the Tongue. On top of that, he was diagnosed with autism when he was a toddler. I don't care what anybody says, and you can call me a conspiracy theorist all you want, but I strongly believe it is connected to an immunization he received. Of course, the government is never going to admit to this, but I know what I know, and unfortunately, he and I both have to live with it.

Don't get me wrong; I love him dearly and I am not complaining, but I'm like any other good parent who wants the best for their children, to include the desire for them to have the quality of life they deserve. He is considered severely autistic, on the nonverbal end of the spectrum, which means he will always need care, need to be kept close and protected in order to be properly cared for and have someone advocate for him. I had to consider every angle of his life, and with his inability to speak it was a no-brainer for me to become self-employed.

Israel started his journey at the CHKD facility in Norfolk, VA with Dr. Craig Derkay. Dr. Derkay was very knowledgeable on this subject matter and performed about three surgeries on Israel's tongue. It hurt me and his dad to try to imagine the pain he had to endure with the hopes of fixing this deformity. I used to feel like I was dying when I bit my tongue, so to have medicine injected with large gauge needles in such a sensitive body part, or laser surgery conducted to cut a part of his tongue off, made us cry.

Israel is by far the one who has inspired me the most and is why I fought to live and overcome every obstacle violently hurled at me or thrown in my path. In his first six years he had four tongue surgeries, was diagnosed with severe autism and a developmental delay. He had to attend several therapy sessions for speech and occupation while keeping up with his medical appointments for follow-up care. Dr. Derkay and the CHKD team did an excellent job in trying to combat the growth that kept coming back, but I could tell they were weary and had run out of options.

Israel had to eat, sleep and try to talk with his tongue hanging out of his mouth. He was stared at and picked on at the daycare he attended because the site was a bit gruesome. There was no way on God's green earth that I could let him go through the rest of his life in this condition, so I prayed and asked for the strength to handle this daunting task and to help me help him.

I took it upon myself to research specialists in the country that specifically dealt with Israel's condition, and there were only two in the whole United States! One was in Washington State and the other was in Richmond, VA. I knew God had answered my prayer, which made strength rise up in me to handle my business. We had to travel frequently for tests, x-rays and surgery prep and this was one of the rare times I was happy that I didn't have a job. Employers will scream they are family-friendly all they want, but if you don't have the time vested to constantly take off, they will have a nice brown box sitting on your desk with all of your belongings neatly packed in it, waiting for you to retrieve it and quietly exit the building. Ask me how I know, LOL.

God provided for me and my family in such a way that I knew without a shadow of a doubt His hand was all over that whole situation. Not only were all of my bills paid, but we had money for gas and food while taking the many trips back and forth. When I first met Dr. Rajanya Petersson, I knew within my spirit she was the one that was going to put an end to my son's suffering. She was thorough, answered all of the questions I had thought of and more, and went above and beyond to show human compassion and hospitality. She could see the apprehension in my eyes when we first met because I didn't want Israel to continue to go through unnecessary pain but was willing to try whatever made sense.

Not only did her and her team exceed my expectations, but they went above and beyond afterwards. To this day, I am happy to say that Israel is able to chew his food better, speak clearer and sing his heart out! His vocabulary has increased tremendously and is able to say four or five words in a sentence. He is extremely intelligent, loves technology and all things music. This was the very miracle I needed in my life to give me the strength to now fight for my own freedom.

I was tired of being a victim and decided I wanted to be a victor, to be an overcomer and to give it my all one more time. This is when I realized I was built Ford tough, and no matter what was thrown at me, I was handling it like a champ. I needed to want it more than anything so I could start thinking and moving towards this better life.

I thought about Samson from the Old Testament and what he did before he went out in a blaze of glory; I asked the Lord to strengthen me one last time to fight for a better life for me and my children.

I thought about Jabez and how I felt like a female version of him; I asked if the Lord saw fit that He would bless me indeed and enlarge my territory, for His hand to be with me, and that He would keep me from evil so that I may not cause pain. I asked for grace, mercy and favor so that I could experience the blessings and promises in His Word and to remove whatever was blocking or hindering my prayers from being answered. I started saying affirmations and speaking more positive words over myself and to myself. I declared out loud what I wanted the government to do to rectify their wrongs; I said this often and I said it daily. I was determined to get my just dues from them; that's how and where my fresh start was going to come from.

I asked for Him to reveal whatever it was that I was doing and to give me a break because I was tired of suffering and couldn't take anymore. I boldly said, "Either show me something better or take my life because I cannot keep living like this." I believe God heard me, had mercy and compassion towards me and rebuked the storm that was hovering over my head, and just as He did for Samson and Jabez, He granted what I had requested and turned my life completely around.

Chapter 10

ONE DAY GOD HEARD MY CRY

If there's one thing I have learned in life so far, it is the power of the spoken word and a made-up mind. The ingredients engrained in resilience, determination and persistence were baked in my spirit on a heat level, so high that it burned off the dross disguised as failures, and impurities hidden behind imposter syndrome. All that I thought of as mistakes, poor judgment, and bad decisions are really what shaped me into the woman I am today and the world-changer I am becoming. What was meant to keep me bound and held back is serving as a launching pad, a catapult even, to propel me to my next level.

I was fueled with passion and desire to get to this life I had often dreamed of, envisioned, and imagined, which pushed me to hold on, to not quit while in the pit, and certainly not to give up or give in. What a major contrast compared to all the doom and gloom confessed in the previous chapters! How is this possible? What was the defining moment that caused this sudden mindset turnaround? It is due to the power of prayer, fervent prayer.

James 5:16 states "...the effectual fervent prayer of a righteous man availeth much." When I read the Bible, there are words that stand out more than others. It causes me to question their meaning, and upon looking up the definition it not only puts the scripture into a deeper context but it makes me understand more and more why it resonated within my spirit. Effectual and fervent... Hmm, let's see what they mean:

Effectual – producing or able to produce a desired or intended result; effective.

Fervent – having or displaying a passionate intensity.

Now let's reread this scripture in an expanded, defined state. "...the effectual (effective) fervent (intense passion) prayer of a righteous man availeth (to be of benefit) much."

Normally, like 99.9% of the time, the verse I read was what I needed in order to deal with whatever situation or circumstance I was experiencing during that particular time. It gave me peace, which allowed me to be calm enough to receive the answer or solution I needed in order to resolve the issue. For many years, I was seeking God for answers and direction. I prayed with fervency, passion and boldness. I wanted a career, I wanted to be successful and I knew I wanted to be the best at whatever I did, but give me something to do. I was tired of feeling purposeless, meaningless and aimlessly walking the earth. Not discounting motherhood, but I wanted to be more than a mother. I was determined to continue to "bug God" until He heard my cries and pleas and answered me. Then, one day, He did.

I was at a bus stop and struck up a conversation with someone who seemed to be an angel in disguise. Somehow, we got on to the subject of me being a veteran and they asked if I was getting any assistance from the military. I said I didn't know I was entitled to anything and they told me to try because you never know. They stated they knew someone who was receiving disability for sinus issues and another for acne, so surely I could think of an ailment I could get paid for. I thought about it and decided to pursue it. After all, what was the worst that could happen besides being told no, right? I went to a local Veteran Affairs office to talk to someone about what I could receive and while standing in line my eyes were drawn to a poster that read three words that ultimately changed my life: Military Sexual Trauma. It proceeded to say that the military recognizes MST has occurred throughout the years and they want to make things right. I felt an excitement rise in me I hadn't felt in years! I knew right then and there that God answered my prayers and He was going to justify the wrongs in His way. I filed the paperwork necessary to get my claim started, and what should have taken a couple of years, God showed me favor and my claim was expeditiously processed within 30 days!

Life changed drastically for me. I received much needed therapy and disability compensation, along with medical benefits. I was able to go back to school at the government's expense—not only me but all of my children as well. Everything I spoke or wrote in my journal concerning the government started to manifest right before my very eyes, and I was ecstatic! I joined a support group with other women who were also survivors of MST, and I started assisting other veterans with whatever help they needed. My time had finally come to begin rebuilding my life one beautiful piece at a time, and I grabbed ahold of it with all my might.

I started to feel different; I felt alive and felt like I had purpose, something I hadn't felt in quite a few years. I was starting to laugh louder, smile harder and open up about my journey. I could feel the desire to live on purpose starting to grow in me, and eventually I let it consume me. I finally had joy, unspeakable joy that the world didn't give, and I certainly wasn't going to let anything and anyone take it away.

I began to look at myself in the mirror with admiration instead of disdain. I could feel self-love rising from the pit of my stomach and clouding over my heart. I didn't want to just throw on whatever to look somewhat decent; no, I got back into my love for fashion and pampering myself. I wanted to undo the damage I had allowed in my body by eating poorly, not exercising, not taking painstaking care of myself like I used to. I even started going back to the salon to get my hair done and kept a fresh manicure and pedicure.

I had fought long and hard to get to this place, and I felt as if God stepped in and started fighting for me. He left no stone unturned as He attended to every need I had, honored my wants and even allowed the desires of my heart to appear. I could not believe that I was seeing and feeling what was a distant dream now becoming everyday life with the promise and assurance of it getting sweeter and sweeter as the days went by.

I am still on my journey of healing as there were many layers that needed to unravel, but I am further along than I was when I started. I learned how to let go of the reins of control and allowed God to be the lover of my soul and the captain of my ship. My voyage to Atlantis has been effervescent, for I have discovered that it is possible to be a masterpiece and a work of art in progress at the same time. The canvas of my life that once appeared blank, dull and lifeless is now a vivacious splash of colors made with haphazard strokes. The beauty of it all is apparent when you take this canvas and turn it just right; the sunlight hits certain angles and the diamond that I am, that was hidden in the rough and underneath the rubble, now shines brilliantly like a prism of rainbow-like colors.

Chapter 11

ON THE ROAD TO RICHES

What I thought was the end of one thing turned out to be the beginning of another, but in a good way. This is where God began to allow things to ease up for me, but not without a few more bumps and bruises. Let me back up for a second—remember what I said about owning my own business, being self-employed, etc.? Well, ever since I left the military, I really didn't have a career. I had a top security clearance in telecommunications as technology was something I was really good at, but, unfortunately, I was robbed of the opportunity to really have a life career in this field. Naturally I am administratively gifted and can manage the hell out of an office building, but it wasn't the actual career path I was aiming for. Anybody can mindlessly shuffle paperwork, but I wanted to do more and be more, so I set out to get exactly what I wanted.

Technically I was back at the drawing board of figuring out what options were out there for minority women. I had to think of something because being a slouch is nowhere located in my DNA. I am a busybody, and I can't help it. I have to be doing something at all times, unless I am relaxing on purpose. I was feeling like anything was possible and I wanted to make moves off of that momentum.

My focus was always to succeed and make lots of money while doing whatever had my name on it, so I did some research to find resources that would help me achieve this goal. I attended a program called Launch Hampton Roads at Old Dominion University in 2012. This is where I learned about the most lucrative industries that needed minority women to participate; construction and transportation were the two that desperately needed this kind of representation, and I was a poster child for it.

What I wasn't told was how male dominated these two industries were, how everyone and their brother's uncle had some sort of construction business in Hampton Roads, and how oversaturated the market was for anyone to get a fair piece of the pie. On top of that, you needed a contractor's license to perform any of the work. Even with knowing this, I didn't let it deter me from pursuing available opportunities. I couldn't get past certain roadblocks so I had to think like a hustler and figure out how I could break into these industries without having to go through the obvious obstacle course. That's when I discovered the world of government contracting and that was all she wrote.

I owe all of the credit to Linda Cramer of Q10 Contracting for she is the one who saw who I was beyond what my circumstances portrayed. She breathed life into me by speaking words of empowerment and encouragement and was not moved by what she knew to be my temporary status. We met in 2012 around the time I started attending the class at ODU. I came to her office on 24th Street in Downtown Norfolk to ask more questions about how government contracting worked and if I could learn how to do it. She took the time to explain more about it, where I fit in, and what the potential payouts were, which piqued my interest even more.

I ate up every word spoken as it gave me a glimmer of hope that I could actually make something of myself. I said, "Wow, I can't believe I am sitting on this fabulous red sofa, talking to someone so accomplished in this field!"

She paused before speaking, looked me squarely in the eyes and said, "Marqueta, you are more accomplished than you know. It's not what we go though in life, but it's how you respond to it. I am looking at a multimillionaire sitting on that fabulous sofa, and I cannot wait to see you achieve it!"

What she said in that moment brought tears to my eyes. I had been so beaten down by life that I would've gladly accepted having a few thousand dollars, but never in my wildest dreams did I think I could see millions. That was the day the passion to succeed was sparked and my desire to rise above and overcome became a personal movement.

She clued me in to the key pieces and components, which became the literal roadmap of information I needed to know, and how to use them to my advantage. I learned about the power of federal contracting and how there were not a lot of minorities who knew of its existence, and certainly not a lot of women in the industries in which I was interested.

Linda continued to break down the different "socioeconomic statuses" and how the government favored these categories. These statuses were based on your nationality, finances and if you served your country; they held veterans and service-disabled veterans in a higher regard.

Let me not breeze past this point right here. When the Bible says that all things work together for our good, it literally means EVERYTHING! When I heard this, I thought I could hear angels singing softly in the background. It all made sense! I could not believe that everything I previously struggled with and suffered from was now becoming a road paved with gold towards all of the promises and riches and wealth engraved with my name on it, just waiting for me to show up and claim it!

I took the time to explain all of this because I don't know whose hands this book will fall into and I always share knowledge with everyone I meet because I understand that certain pieces of information can change the seasons of your life. Who knew that any of this was available when it was not being openly advertised? I have been perfecting this concept since 2013 and have also been educating, empowering and encouraging other people through my consulting business regarding how to get into this same position.

The day I found out I qualified for millions of dollars' worth of work is the day my life changed and would never be the same. I could now fulfill every single dream, vision and goal I was able to muster up the strength to conceive in my mind and actually believe that in the midst of everything I was going through there was a possibility of a better life. I was determined to hold on long enough to achieve this.

Once I learned that I was in a special category as a veteran and how much money I could make, it was on from there! All I saw were the potential dollar signs I would make and went full throttle from there. I just knew that being armed with this knowledge I was about to run the world in a matter of months, but boy was I wrong. I had developed a thick skin for surviving the military and surviving the hood but being self-employed or an entrepreneur was a different kind of wild animal, and I was in for the taming of my life.

Chapter 12

MY PLANS MADE GOD LAUGH HYSTERICALLY

Construction was the arena I wanted to play in first; I devised a plan of action to tackle this first then move on to something else. I thought all I needed to do was be in the right places at the right time, say a few charming words and I would have the best of the best eating out of the palm of my hand. I was the purple unicorn in terms of business that had everything a construction business owner needed. The dollar signs that danced in my head had me on a natural high every day. I started thinking differently, moving methodically, and planned for the avalanche of dollars that was about to hit my life.

My plan was to go after construction opportunities in Hampton Roads and then venture out to other states along the East Coast. Eventually I would seek to partner on other projects in the Midwest, West Coast and finally other parts of the world. I planned on securing the deals then finding the labor to get the job done. I was bringing my assets to the table and everyone involved would eat lovely. After all of the expenses and payroll was paid,

I would take my cut, my partners would take theirs, and then I would rinse and repeat. Easy peasy, right? Wrong!

The good ol' Commonwealth of Virginia has more laws on everything that benefits the lawmakers. There is so much red tape surrounding anything that is meant for advancement that it makes it virtually impossible to get what you need done, if you don't know the right people or your money is funny. I'm not saying this is everyone's gripe or that this is everyone's story, but as a minority, if you don't have Daddy Warbucks' type money then you have no choice but to get it from the mud, which has caused many to walk away from their dreams because they can't catch a break.

I needed a contractor's license, which meant taking a class, which meant more time would pass causing a wedge between me and my big money dreams. I had to think of a way around this; I did research, asked questions and found out I personally didn't need the license but someone on my team did. I took this information and ran a marathon with it! I set out to attend every networking event there was from New York all the way down to Atlanta. I sought out every event that was centered around construction or the federal marketplace so that I could immerse myself deeper. I did this from 2012 until 2018 until I couldn't take anymore no's, or doors slammed in my face, or being laughed at for being a woman who was dogmatic about her dreams.

My vivid imagination pictured me showing my plans to God with all the bells and whistles attached, like I was presenting to the Dukes Brothers from the movie *Trading Places*. I have on my three-piece navy-blue power suit, standing tall and confident in my Louboutin stilettos giving a mean, full-on PowerPoint presentation with the sound effects, transition slides, the whole nine yards. I'm speaking eloquently, enunciating my words correctly, and killing them with my expansive vocabulary, thinking He is going to nod His head in approval, say, "Well done, Daughter of Eve, let's show the world what you're made of," and then … boom! I'm a mogul out here doing big things and what not. But no, that's now quite how it went. I think God and the angels waited until I was done and laughed hysterically at my plans. I mean kicking and screaming, with tears streaming down their faces type of laughing. I felt like He said, "Oh, this is too cute," and snatched my proposal from me, hurled it across heaven's board room and it perfectly landed in the trash!

I was sitting on my bed, crying my eyes out because I had to let go of my desire to have a construction-services-based business. I had incessantly tried since 2012 to see this dream manifest, and the only project I was given was a residential job worth $4,286. That was it! Out of six years, that was the best I could do, and I felt like crap.

Different scenarios replayed in my mind and made me mad as hell because I knew I put my all into everything I did! I thought about every email I sent with my company's information to market myself from California to Canada.

Every phone call I made that made me feel like a stalker because I called several times to show how interested I was and that all I needed was a chance to showcase my skills.

Every meeting I ran to, sometimes with no gas in my tank, thinking this was the meeting that was going to change my life, only to be told I didn't have enough skin in the game yet.

All of the Lunch and Learns I had to overdraft my account to attend, just so I could rub elbows with the female movers and shakers in construction that I thought for sure would look out, but they brushed me off because they didn't recognize my company name.

I always go above and beyond when I set my mind to really achieve a thing, but it looked like all of my hard work was disappearing right before my very eyes. I had tried for a few years to get a contractor's license, which was needed to go after local projects, but the only place I could afford had canceled again and had the nerve to say they were doing away with the class in general. I was mad as hell because no matter what I did, or how hard I pursued or attempted, I failed.

I was mad at myself for believing I could be something great and angry that I put so much time, energy and money into seeing this vision launch yet it left me with nothing to show for my hard work, or at least that's what I was beginning to think. I could feel depression trying to sneak up on me and knew I needed to do something to shake it off. Otherwise, I would be going right back to where I had been healed from, and I couldn't afford for that to happen.

The best way to get over personal problems is to help someone with theirs, and that's exactly what I set out to do. I thought about what my business coaches instilled and me and decided to put some of what I learned to use. They said to ask questions out loud and the answers will come. I started affirming in question mode. "Who needs my help? What do I have that I can sell? What do I know that will help other people? What is a need I can provide a solution for, or what are the problems that need tangible and physical actions to provide answers?"

I have always been a team player and I thrive on seeing other people win. I want everyone to win, which is why I do what I do. Not long after I asked the questions, the answer came to me. The mayor of the city I grew up in, Mayor Kenny Alexander, emailed me out of the blue and told me about a program that helps inmates while they are incarcerated and thought I would be a good fit. I called the contact information listed and inquired about this program. I met with one of the directors, for lunch and learned more about this exciting program.

The Norfolk Sheriff's Office called it Pathways as it was geared towards creating a path by helping inmates learn a trade or a skill so when they were released from incarceration, they could implement what they learned and potentially give themselves a better life. This would also create a domino effect that would not only affect them but their children and families as well as the communities in which they would reside. Our tax dollars go towards taking care of those in the penal systems, so why not help them as much as possible to be successful as returning citizens in order to be able to become re-acclimated into society? Truth be told, everyone has done something in their lives that warranted a jail or prison sentence, but some of us were blessed not to get caught or be punished in this manner.

I immediately saw how I fit into the puzzle because no one else was teaching this information. I told him what I did as a consultant and all that I had learned along the way, so it made total sense to teach them the business side of things in case they wanted to take the learned skills to another level. He asked me to elaborate, and I laid the game down flat! I have the ability to learn complex things and break them down into laymen's terms. I explained how the minutest details could hold a person up longer than normal all because there is no understanding or no one takes the time to explain it. He was beyond impressed and definitely agreed that I was the missing piece.

I met with the rest of the team in a boardroom type interview. I went armed with visual aids explaining what I was going to teach and the purpose that it served. My handouts were neatly packaged in folders with pens to write notes, my business card and a short bio about my background. I promised God that I would do things in excellence, no matter how small the task or assignment was, so when He blessed me with a big opportunity, I would do it right.

I was still a little salty about what I perceived as a failure and would have my downtrodden moments, but I pushed it out of my mind and shook it off when the first day came to meet my students. I told the staff I would teach both males and females, with no more than 15 people in each session. The plan was to meet once a week for eight weeks unless something came up. The irony of this is that I used to go to this same jail years ago, visiting different people who were locked up for various crimes. I was on the other side of the plexiglass window talking to them on a phone, having to talk in code because the nature of our conversation was nowhere near law-abiding.

Now here I was, face-to-face with different people locked up for various crimes but talking to them freely and *teaching* them how to be law-abiding. I treated them with the dignity and respect they deserved; I never referred to them as what they temporarily were, inmates, but I spoke to who they permanently were as human beings, as individuals who didn't need further condemnation but more validation.

I referred to them as Mr. or Ms., and whatever their last name was. I humbly greeted them when they came in but confidently commandeered the room. I wasn't afraid or scared of who they were, nor their crimes; none of that mattered to me because I was used to being around folks like that, but the biggest reason is that I knew what it felt like for someone to pass judgment on you without knowing the full story. I intentionally didn't ask why they were there because I didn't want anything to cloud my viewpoint of them in case I personally knew whomever their crimes affected. I will admit that I was nervous to a degree because it was something I had never done, but God assured me that I could do it, so I took it very seriously in order for Him to be seen through me.

I dressed in business attire to bring what I taught to life. We did an assignment in which we pretended we were at a networking event each class, and each of them described their attire. That's what they "wore" in class as opposed to the gray and black jumpsuits they had on.

I expounded on how to display business etiquette in any type of business environment, complete with name tents they positioned in front of them just as they would at a networking event. I could see that this made them feel important even if it was a slight gesture.

I created a class curriculum and gave them a copy. It outlined what they were going to learn and how they could use it in everyday life as well as business. I fully engaged each of them in class letting them know that I taught in a participatory manner, rather than just lecturing.

They had homework from the reading materials I gave them. I had to improvise with the limitations imposed on what I could bring in from the outside, but the staff was gracious enough to print anything I needed, no matter the quantity, so I would send excerpts from books I suggested they read when they were released, but for classroom purposes we focused on specific chapters. I wanted to expand their minds beyond what they knew and what they saw, shifting their focus and perspective at the same time.

We studied the Universal Laws and rested on the Law of Attraction. They were especially excited about doing an actual vision and dream board and how it would change their lives. We discussed the difference between the two so they would have more clarity when they created their own. I was allowed to bring in my own magazines since they didn't have staples, which brought their projects to life. To see something in color as opposed to black and white can really make a difference. We don't think about these small subtleties until we no longer have the privilege of accessing them.

Graduation day came and I was beyond thrilled! I saw hope dancing like embers of fire in their eyes, and I was grateful to know I played a part in making this happen. When they first came, they were listless and only wanted to take the class to have something to pass the time. They didn't know I came armed with an arsenal of life-altering knowledge, and once you heard it you couldn't unhear it, and they had no choice but to accept the inadvertent challenge they were now posed with to make some serious changes. They had made major strides over the course of the eight weeks and I was so damn proud of each of them.

Y'all already know how I went about planning for this; I did it as big as I they would let me. I placed a request for dessert (something only the staff received in the cafeteria), coffee (which apparently is a hot commodity, no pun intended) and punch. I had a guest speaker come in to deliver words of encouragement and empowerment, like a real commencement. Rev. Dr. Kirk T. Houston, Sr. who is the senior pastor of Gethsemane Community Fellowship Baptist Church in Norfolk, VA, spoke with such passion and inspiration that some of the males said they were going to visit when they were released. This made my heart swell with so much joy; what if this was the reason behind me being a willing vessel to teach business basics? What if it was to save at least one and that one would go on to do great things in the world?

Whatever the purpose was, it was divinely orchestrated for Dr. Houston to even make an appearance. He already had clearance to visit inside the jail from a program he was currently running, but I didn't know it at the time. It just so happened that I was seated next to him at a retirement party for one of the deputies, and I felt the urge to ask if he would be my guest speaker. He asked what the date was and when I told him, he said it was ironic that his medical appointment on that same date was cancelled earlier that day and that he would lock me in before his assistant filled that opening with something else. God is so amazing at how He weaves all things together!

I knew I had made an impact when Dr. Houston called me later on and commended me on the class. The graduates had a chance to come up and give their comments or expressions on the class and what they learned. He was supposed to leave for another appointment but felt inclined to stay and listen to what they had to say, even if that meant he would be late. I was honored that he thought enough of me and them to push his schedule up, knowing how much he stayed in demand throughout the Hampton Roads area.

He said, "Young lady, in the twenty plus years that I have been mentoring and interacting with the inmates, especially the males, I have never seen them light up or even act as if they were impressed by anything anyone did, and that impressed me. Keep doing what you are doing by freely pouring into others and watch how God will bless you!"

I thanked him over and over again for the kind remarks and got off the phone before I broke down and cried in his ear. I really didn't think it was that big of a deal; I know I'm a people person and I love to be of some sort of service to them, but to hear those words spoken from someone who is very well-known and has borne witness to things I can only imagine, that meant the world to me.

Word spread throughout the jail about the business class taught by this "fine-ass sistah who dresses really nice and always smells amazing" and I was in demand. The deputies were asking the inmates questions about me, wanting to know who I was and where I came from, but were too intimidated to ask. They used to have me cracking up when they repeated the comments and said I had the whole jail buzzing. It felt good to hear and gave my ego a much-needed booster. I went home that night, looked myself in the mirror and said, "Girl, you bad as hell!"

I stayed focused on the task at hand and never took anyone up on the many offers to take me out. I didn't want my reputation to be tainted or stained in any way, which would undo the impact I had made up to that point. Men are still men, even with a uniform on, and I refused to have stories made up behind a simple cup of coffee. I was on a mission to change lives and was going to do just that. I was on a roll teaching my second cohort and thinking of a way I could accommodate my wait list when COVID-19 hit and shut the entire … world … completely … down.

Chapter 13

HE WHO BEGAN A GOOD WORK IN ME

I don't know why the drawing board couldn't find someone else to stalk and leave me alone, but the way my life was set up, we were glued at the hips whether I liked it or not. I had been back in its face so many times and was determined to leave stronger and wiser than the previous breakups. This time it wasn't just me, but it was every human being on planet Earth as the coronavirus swept across the nation and the globe, affecting everything in its path.

The year 2020 was supposed to be one where everything lined up like perfect vision. Churches had made up bold affirmations, people were determined to really stick to their resolutions for sure, and everyone was amped at what the beginning of the new decade meant. Here this is February and it looked like everything and everyone was going to hell in a handbasket, soaked in gasoline with rockets underneath!

There was so much uncertainty, no one knew what to do or what to expect. I had run out of options and couldn't think about anything else except keeping my family safe. I don't think anyone knew how serious it was; all anyone could do was to gather as much information as they could by being glued to the television. That's when the death tolls started climbing, and fear gripped the viewers. I amped up my prayers even more and said, "Lord, surely you are not going to let me go out like this! What about your promises to me? I haven't even seen the good life yet! God, please tell me or show me something. I refuse to accept this!"

He brought back a memory I had forgotten about from a couple years back, and I knew that was His way of answering me. I remember standing by the banister in my bedroom when I made a verbal declaration that even in the moment I spoke it, I felt my life shift in the direction of what I said. I don't know what made me look into a construction opportunity in Houston, TX, but I did and that's when everything started to change.

My mind traveled back to September 2018. I was standing by the banister in my attic-turned-bedroom, speaking to Abel Garcia who is in charge of something like a Houston chapter for minority contractors. I expressed what my interests were, where I was located and what the possibilities were of me working on a project there. He took the time to explain the ins and outs and when we were nearing the end of the call, he started to talk about all the great things this city had to offer. I listened intently and was so drawn in that I started to picture myself in this wonderful place he was passionately describing but quickly lost the reverie. He posed a challenging question about relocating and I immediately thought of a thousand and one reasons why I couldn't ... I shouldn't ... therefore, I wouldn't.

Hampton Roads was my comfort zone; I knew where everything was, I was close to friends and family and I had created business roots that I was intent on seeing grow full term. There was nothing on this side of Earth that was going to stand in the way of me seeing all of the blood, sweat and tears that I poured into chasing my dreams, visions and goals since 2012 come to fruition. I somewhat rattled off a few things on my "Reasons Why I Should Stay Put" checklist when he asked me to do something odd. He asked me to repeat after him and say one simple sentence: "If it is God's plan for my life, I will move to Houston, TX." He had me say it at least three times and then said, "I can't wait until you move here," before hanging up.

It took me a few minutes to gather myself because I felt strange afterwards and even questioned, *What in the world did I just say or do?* I shrugged it off and kept going about my day but couldn't shake the conversation from my head for anything. Days turned into weeks and all of my attempts to get back into the business swing of things kept falling to the wayside; nothing seemed to work out like it normally did before and it was agitating me to no end.

Fast forward to the present moment I was thinking of the memory, I also started seeing the numbers "1004" in different variations. I would see it when I needed to check the time, I saw it on license plates, and I saw it on documents. It happens to be my birthday as well. I have a spiritual aptitude for understanding the biblical meaning of numbers as well as intuitively knowing they are used as signs to catch my attention. When God needs to get a message across to me, this is one of the methods He uses.

So now that my attention was caught, I began to seek God for the meaning and instructions. I knew there was a reason behind it, but I needed to know why and what I was supposed to do with the information. By now it was November of 2018 and I had to make what seemed like a painful decision. I calmed myself and stilled my spirit so I could pray and tune my ears in spiritually. He didn't readily answer me, but I kept getting in my prayer closet every day until He did. He gave me one word: transportation. I let it resonate within my mind and soul and when I felt a blanket of peace cover me, I knew this was the game changer.

Before I make any moves, I always do my due diligence in research so that I can avoid pitfalls and unnecessary mistakes. I am a perfectionist to a fault; I need to know everything so that I can make calculated decisions, especially when it is a new venture. I didn't have anyone I could ask who would run the game down flat, so I had no choice but to trust that God would provide all of the answers I needed. I have come across so many people who would rather see you fail than give you one tidbit of information that could change your life. That's when things started happening quick and fast.

I started connecting to people in other states who were forthcoming with all of the information I needed and answered every question with no problems. Before I knew it, I had a complete plan of action with step-by-step details on what to do, who to call and how to proceed afterwards. I changed the name of my business because I felt like the other one was mud in the business world; however, I kept the logo, a Phoenix bird, because of what it metaphorically represents: rising out of fiery ashes. That was me all day as I can relate 100%. On December 31st, 2019, Phoenix Global Group, LLC was formed before the stroke of midnight.

Since there was an indefinite timeframe as to when anyone would return to buildings for work, I didn't question when the program would start back up and took that time to start making an exit strategy. I knew Houston was where I was being led, but I was second-guessing what I heard and decided to try my hand at staying close to home. I was thinking of either Maryland or Atlanta.

Although I had set up a new business, I felt like I needed to table my goal of being self-employed until the world was figured out and get back into corporate America. By now I was way more stable than I had been in years and didn't have the same issues that affected my employment before, so I could wait somewhat patiently on what to do with the newly formed biz. I had transportation, a steady income and my kids were older. This was a recipe for success for sure and went about doing the opposite of what I was instructed to do.

I set my plan in motion, intently determined to make it work. If I moved to Maryland, I was going to apply for a job working *for* the government as opposed to *with* as a contractor. One of my closest friend's, Marvette Liggins, who has been more like a sister for the last 40 years of my life, lived there and had been begging me for years to move up there to be close by her. I thought to myself she was about to get her wish, and that worked for me because I wanted to be near family.

My second option was Atlanta and the ONLY reason why that was even a thought was due to two of my sons. They are both gifted in the arts, singing, acting, dancing, the spoken word, songwriting and scriptwriting. I figured I would use my wily ways to get connected to Tyler Perry and be a momager like Kris Kardashian. It was not what I wanted, but I had convinced myself that my time was up, I was a washed-up has-been, and I might as well help them be great since, clearly, I wasn't going to be.

Mind you, I kept hearing Houston buzzing in my spirit, and like a nagging fly, I swatted the thought away. I know what I heard, but I wanted to put fleeces before God to see which route I should take. Besides, who moves halfway across the country by themselves anyway? I had made a few moves like this before and after a short time had to come right back to VA; I knew this wasn't one of those times, but I needed to make sure because, this time, I had a feeling I wasn't coming back.

One of my connections in MD told me that a position had just opened up and that I needed to hurry up and apply before it went public. I was a major candidate for this job with my veteran status as that's what they were looking for. She pretty much assured me that I had the job but still had to do the preliminary stuff of filling out all of the required documents. I was convinced this was the best move for me; I would only be three hours away from my kids' dad and from my family. I was far enough that you couldn't just pop up but not too far away from what I knew and what I was familiar with.

It was all figured out; now all I needed to do was call my sister and tell her the good news, but she had a bit of news to tell me herself. Although we're very close, we would sometimes go months without talking and when we did, we picked up right where we left off at. I was smiling so hard thinking she was about to scream in glee at my good news of leaving Virginia and moving to Maryland, but instead she dropped a major bomb on me. She told me she had moved to Chicago just a couple of months ago for ministry purposes, and was never returning back to Maryland if she could help it.

My mouth was wide open. I could not believe what I was hearing. She had lived in Annapolis for almost twenty years with no signs of moving anywhere, much less that freezing cold state, and when I decided to move there, she was already gone. Maryland is way more expensive than Virginia, and I was going to need to stay with her a few months to save up enough to move out. I think God knew I was going to try my hand, so He stirred things up in the background just to make sure I did things His way in the long run.

After we finished talking—well, after she scolded me for trying to pull a fast one, knowing I am gifted prophetically to see and hear when God speaks or moves and to obey where He is sending me—she encouraged me not to be afraid for if He was sending me, then He was going to go before me to prepare the way and clear my path.

I thanked her, got off the phone and went into my prayer closet to ask God for yet another sign. He led me to Genesis 12:1–3 and that was all I needed to let go of the fear and doubt and, for once in my life, completely trust Him and His plans for me.

I prayed for radical faith so that I would not waver on my decision, no matter what I saw or heard, but of course the only way I would find out if I had radical faith was to be tested in it.

By now it was April and virus cases were being reported with skyrocketing numbers in different cities, Houston being one of the main ones. I had to stop watching the news and the reports the media was constantly forcing us to see. I was also keeping quiet about the move until I had to say something to my loved ones. I knew they wouldn't understand because my choice to move would affect them in more ways than one, but it was imperative that I only thought about saving me and my younger children, not anyone else. I had become too much of a crutch, trying to fix issues and problems that were beyond my control, and enough was enough. Too many times we stand in God's way of how He chooses to parent His children. I was guilty of doing this but not anymore.

The one incident that shook me to the core was the passing of my next-door neighbor. I saw him the evening before cutting grass, and early the next morning he was being brought out on a stretcher, struggling to breathe. It looked like a scene from out of a movie; EMT workers were garbed in quarantine garments from head to toe, police officers had on face shields with masks and gloves and were instructing everyone to stay at least six feet away. His wife looked so distraught and didn't know what to do since they wouldn't let her ride with him in the ambulance; then she got in her car to follow it to the hospital.

There was an eerie hush over my street after the fire trucks, police cars and ambulance had left. I kept wondering what in the world happened next door that all of that was even needed. It wasn't even an hour later when I saw his wife pull up. We had had small friendly conversations here and there, so I didn't feel out of place to go talk to her. I asked if Allen was okay, and she shook her head no. She was talking to me through the glass screen door, which I thought was odd, but I quickly understood why after her next sentence. She started crying and told me he had died from the virus, and that's why she was keeping her distance in case she might be infected.

I felt like someone had snatched the welcome mat I was standing on from underneath me. I was in disbelief from what I heard her say, but I couldn't move. I didn't know what to say. What do you say to someone who loses a loved one in less than 60 minutes of being by their side? When I found my voice, I told her to let me know if she needed anything, offered my condolences and left. I think I sat motionless for about two hours from total shock. It's not that I didn't believe what was being said about the virus and how quickly people were passing, but it hits different when you see it with your own eyes and so close to home, literally.

When I finally collected my wits, I told God there was no way I heard Him correctly with this move. Not after what I had just witnessed … no sir, absolutely not! I went on a rant and rave and said every church saying that came to mind about the devil being a whole lie and the truth ain't in him. I went to rebuking the thought that was even planted in my head about the move; I mean the whole nine yards! Fear was gripping me and doubt was knocking me upside my head so badly that I called my prayer partners Nikkia Tolbert and Tammara Britt, crying and asking them to intercede for me. After they prayed, I had enough peace to cover my racing thoughts and still my spirit.

I asked God to make it plain and clear to me about this move because I would be devastated if I lost my life or one of my kids to this virus due to being out of place. He led me to Isaiah 41:10 and after I read the scripture, I knew I could safely make the move and everything would be more than alright. There were a few more signs He showed me to keep assuring me that I was in His perfect will to make this transition. On June 28th, 2020, I packed up my belongings and my younger children and drove halfway across the United States to my new beginning. I arrived in Houston on July 1st, completing the trek and ready to start my new life.

From the moment I touched down in this amazing city, God performed miracle after miracle and opened door after door on my behalf. Everything I lost previously, God gave me double. The connections I've been making far outweigh the ones I left behind. I started meeting people that were strategically placed and inserted at the very moment I needed them. Me and my younger three children were in a hotel for 40 days and nights because it took some time for my housing to get situated, but during that time I had so much peace and didn't want for anything! When I finally found a place, it was in a prominent neighborhood that is almost an exact replica of Stonebridge Crossing in Norfolk, VA.

During my hotel stay I kept seeing a challenge for a media opportunity flash across my social media pages. I felt the urge to click on it to see what it was about, and to this day I am so happy I didn't allow the lack of self-confidence to talk me out of what proved to be a major move for me. This challenge allowed me to be mentored by media personality Chris Winfield and his fiancée Jen Gottlieb. Jen used to host a show on MTV and is a Broadway actress, and Chris has appeared on almost every popular news network, magazine and daytime talk shows, just to name a few.

These two, along with a couple of other accountability partners, encouraged and empowered me to not only get this book finished, but educated me on how to share my testimony across the platform that started growing for me. My first major client was Dom Faussette, owner of *ThinkReactLead*. Dom is an Executive Coach and Leadership Speaker currently pursuing after government contracts with my assistance. Brenda Warren, an author notably known as "The Soulutionist" interviews high level performers from the United States and other countries. She is a mindset coach and speaks on platforms internationally. Not only is she my accountability partner and veteran sister, but she is also one of the greatest friends anyone could ever hope for.

I learned so much from Chris and Jen as they certainly paved the path that was part of my destiny, but I could only go but so far with them. Don't get me wrong, they are extremely kind and humble, and never made me feel inferior to them. They also equipped me with media leads and contacts out of this world, but I needed more intimate coaching to really know how to market myself and since they stay in high demand, it was virtually impossible to get the hands-on guidance I desired, so I asked God to lead me to someone who could help me further.

When I met Monique Jackson, the PR guru for Def Jam records, I knew instantly she was my next destiny connect, which further confirmed that I am on the right track with the media part of my brand. During our first conversation she said, "Oh girl, you need to let me coach you! You have way too much in you that people need to hear, and it's too many folks out here that you can help." She launched her coaching program, "$he's a Millionaire" just a few short weeks afterwards, and I was one of the first in the cohort to sign up. I know this investment is going to skyrocket my life to the levels already designed and in place for me to go.

I don't want to make it seem like everything has been all roses since I've been in Houston. I remember I heard the words "accelerated growth" while in prayer one evening, and I thought it was a word of encouragement for my prayer partners, not knowing it was for me. I didn't realize how far behind I was in personal and professional development, but I quickly found out. Shortly after I heard those words, I went through a major healing that went so deep internally, I didn't think I was going to make it through.

I felt like I was in the Twilight Zone for a couple months as I physically felt the effects from the emotional and mental healing taking place that was long overdue. Oddly, I was at peace while being tossed to and fro, from the ebbs and flows of the currents that carried me deep into the waters of healing. When it felt as if I would drown in the depths of this convalescent sea, I was brought back to the shore of resuscitation, only for this song and dance to be my daily norm until the song faded, and dance ended. I felt rejuvenated, revived and restored in areas I didn't even know existed anymore. I even lost a great deal of weight that stemmed from all of the emotional baggage I was carrying around for years; not only did I feel happy and healthy, I *looked* as if I was 20 years younger!

The intensity of this healing went underneath all of the trauma and pain that hadn't been dealt with properly and uprooted everything so that I could purge it out. As painful as it was, I let God do whatever needed to be done so that I could move on and not have to revisit. Thank God I made it through and I have been elevating and vibrating on higher frequencies ever since. Once the healing process was over, opportunities started popping up left and right. I did a couple of interviews with The Sheila Mac Show, and Pantea Kalhor on how to thrive with PTSD. I have been invited to speak on a few platforms and podcasts which have led to business deals, and I have made more money in these last six months than I have in the last three years combined!

My purpose has been renewed and everything I need, want and desire has been rushing towards me without delay. Although media is something of a dormant dream coming alive, God is also showing me that everything I learned about contracting and consulting was all going to come together and propel me into places I never knew would be possible. I connected with not one but two heavy hitters in the federal marketplace and they have been pouring major knowledge into me, shaping me into more of the beast I already am.

The whole purpose for my existence was to be the beacon of light for all to see, so they could know if God did it for me He can and will certainly do it for you! He has blessed me with opportunities to share my story of being an overcomer in media outlets that reach millions of households. He has equipped me with the skills, knowledge and wisdom to help others launch their businesses by helping them navigate through the business world and hold their hand during the process. Who but God could heal my mind enough to even think and provide solutions on this level? It's all God; I give Him all the glory!

Knowing what I know now about the spiritual giftings the Holy Spirit blessed me to house, I am extremely grateful I didn't forfeit the blessings and rewards God had in store for me by taking my own life because my life was just that hard. He already knew what I was going to endure and I wholeheartedly believe that He favored me with unmerited grace and mercy when so many others have lost their lives going through the same struggles I did, yet I'm still standing and still pushing against all odds and in spite of what it looks like.

As I bring this testimony of God's grace, mercy and goodness over my life to an end, I am still in awe that I have made it this far and am able to share it with you, my friend. Who knows that Something Beautiful could come from all of the ugliness, turmoil and hideousness I endured? Who but God could put together a plan so elaborate for my life out of what looked like a ball of chaos and confusion?

I used to always ask the question, "Why Me, Lord?"

When I finally got to a place where I could hear Him speak, He answered quietly and gently, "Why not you?" We often wonder why we go through what we do in life, but as Believers we have an obligation to "deny ourselves" and take up our crosses designed for us to bear.

Now I know why. The lightbulb finally lit up. I wholeheartedly know that not only was I called, but I am chosen for this. I was built "Ford Tough" for this. God's strength was made perfect in my weakness in this; therefore, I am stronger than ten men as I carry the weight of my earthly assignment with ease. I can honestly say I am so grateful to be in the land of the living where once I dreamed of being dead because that was the only way I believed I would experience peace.

Friend, if for nothing else, my Heavenly Father has made something beautiful of me just so that He could show you He is more than capable and able to make something beautiful out of your life as well. Can I help you a little bit more? I learned early on that we deal with life's challenges for one of two reasons: it was due to a choice we made or God chose us to endure the trial for someone else. His ways and thoughts are so much higher than ours, so whatever He leads us to, He will be with us to see us through.

My future is extremely bright and I'm just now beginning to scratch the surface. Like fingernail in place, eyeing the new furniture to see where I want to scratch type of beginning. The fact that I made it to this point is a testimony in and of itself as you've read. If you would've asked me twenty-something years ago if I knew this is what God had in store for me, I probably would have laughed and cried hysterically, thinking the person asking this was just a delusional as I was at the time. I mean it makes no sense at all that anyone who has endured as many hardships, trials, tribulations, sufferings, struggles … did I leave anything out? But it makes no absolute sense that I even made it this far, and life is truly beginning over for me at this very moment.

I say this with confidence because the choices I made or situations I became entangled in could only have been covered under the blood of Jesus! Nothing else! Friend, I say this in all confidence; if God could take what was a hot mess of my life and turn it into something so brilliantly beautiful then SURELY He can do the same for you! I don't care what it looks like **right now**, I don't care what you've done **in the past**, and I certainly don't agree that you have **no future:** I can assure you that God can take nothing and make something out of it because anything is possible for those who believe. Let Go and Let God make something beautiful out of your life too. Hold on. It's not over. I promise you—the best is YET to come!

ABOUT THE AUTHOR

Marqueta (Negron, Harris) is from Norfolk, VA and grew up in the Berkley section of South Norfolk. She attended Norfolk State University before relocating to Houston, TX to pursue her dreams of entrepreneurship in consulting and government contracting.

She is the mother of six children and two grandchildren and the "fun aunt" to a host of nieces and nephews. She is also the oldest grandchild of sixty plus grand and great-grandchildren, all descendants of Chester Lee and Goldie Jenkins of Ahoskie, NC.

Marqueta is a service-disabled Army veteran who volunteers with various DAV (Disabled American Veteran) chapters to assist other veterans in overcoming adversity and limiting barriers, to help them achieve living their best lives. She also participated in the Norfolk Sheriff's Office program teaching business basics and small business entrepreneurship to both the male and female population with the sole intention to combat recidivism and reincarceration.

Although Marqueta has many spiritual giftings, she knows who she is prophetically, and to whom she belongs, and doesn't need a title to define or validate her kingdom assignment. Through all of the bumps, bruises, trials and struggles experienced in life, she learned that God doesn't call the qualified; instead, He qualifies the called, which boosted her confidence to know that not only is she called but most definitely chosen as an Ambassador for Christ. Marqueta has many scriptures that she loves as they always give her strength and guidance, but her favorite scripture is 1 Cor 9:22: "When I am with those who are weak, I share their weakness, for I want to bring the weak to Christ. Yes, I try to find common ground with everyone, doing everything I can to save some." NLT